SEARCHING FOR HIGHER EDUCATION LEADERSHIP

SEARCHING FOR HIGHER EDUCATION LEADERSHIP

Advice for Candidates and Search Committees

Jean A. Dowdall

 AMERICAN COUNCIL ON EDUCATION
PRAEGER
Series on Higher Education

Library of Congress Cataloging-in-Publication Data

Dowdall, Jean A.
   Searching for higher education leadership : advice for candidates and search committees /
by Jean A. Dowdall.
      p. cm. — (ACE/Praeger series on higher education)
   Includes bibliographical references and index.
   ISBN 0–275–99146–6 (alk. paper)
   1. College administrators—Selection and appointment—United States. I. Title.
LB2331.6952.D69   2007
378.1'10973—dc22   2006038813

British Library Cataloguing in Publication Data is available.

Library of Congress Catalog Card Number: 2006038813
ISBN-10: 0–275–99146–6
ISBN-13: 978–0–275–99146–3

First published in 2007

Praeger Publishers, 88 Post Road West, Westport, CT 06881
An imprint of Greenwood Publishing Group, Inc.
www.praeger.com

Printed in the United States of America

The paper used in this book complies with the
Permanent Paper Standard issued by the National
Information Standards Organization (Z39.48–1984).

10 9 8 7 6 5 4 3 2 1

TO GEORGE

and

TO NINA, ROB, OLIVIA, AND NATHAN

CONTENTS

PREFACE

The search for higher education leadership contributes to shaping the future of higher education. The kinds of leaders we seek, and the way in which we identify and screen and recruit them, will have effects for generations. The search process has been a fascination for me since I was first interviewed by search committees as my career began, then served as a member and later a chair of committees, and then appointed search committees and received their recommendations. As a search consultant since 1996, I built on 25 years of experience in higher education as a faculty member and an administrator. The powerful and inspiring aspirations of higher education that are invoked when new leaders are sought, and the mundane mechanics of organizing the search process, come together in the work of search consultants. I have been privileged to work with many outstanding client institutions, each making its distinctive contribution to American higher education, and with hundreds of talented and dedicated candidates looking for opportunities to be of service.

My interest in writing this book grew out of the belief that both candidates and search committees could be more effective. I am convinced that many candidates for higher education leadership positions are more capable than they appear to be in the search process. I wanted to provide advice that would help them be better prepared and more successful in each search they entered. Similarly, after supporting dozens of searches as a consultant, I thought that search committees could be more effective if they adopted an orderly but flexible process that allowed them to focus attention on learning more about and attracting the best candidates, and less on grappling with procedures. I wanted to offer committees advice that could enhance the search process and lead to more successful conclusions.

INTRODUCTION

The search process for higher education leaders is complex and at times even mysterious for both search committees and candidates. Both are eager for advice about typical search processes and approaches, and about the difficult and controversial situations that can arise. This book focuses on searches for executive positions in higher education administration, and should be useful whether the reader's focus in on searches for presidents, chancellors, or vice presidents/vice chancellors for academic affairs, student affairs, advancement, enrollment or finance. Readers from a range of institutions—elite national research and liberal arts institutions, regional comprehensive institutions, public and private institutions—will all find advice here.

Advice will be offered for candidates (Part I of the book) and for search committees (Part II), and each may find it valuable to consider the issues of concern to the other. Some readers will want to read through the appropriate part of the book, while others will want to use it more like a reference work, seeking specific information or answers to particular questions—e.g., candidates can read about preparing for interviews, or search committees can read about making reference calls.

Part I: Advice for Candidates

Part I focuses on candidates, moving chronologically through a typical search. Before entering a search (the focus of Chapter 1), it is important to know when you are ready to begin looking for a senior leadership role, and how to go about pursuing the opportunities that interest you.

Once a candidate has decided to apply for a position, there is a vast array of choices to be made with regard to the materials you will submit. Chapter 2 considers how best to shape your cover letter, curriculum vitae, and list of references so that they are most effective in representing you during the search process.

Those whose application materials are attractive to the search committee will typically be invited for a preliminary interview. Candidates have only an hour to two to convince the search committee that they deserve further attention. Chapter 3 explores the dynamics of these interviews and suggests ways to prepare for them.

Chapter 4 takes up the grueling but revealing second-round interview, which may be an open public event on campus, or a closed event for a select group of institutional representatives. A few candidates are invited to come to campus and meet with the potential supervisor, colleagues, supervisees and others whose positions are linked to the one being filled. Every moment from arrival to departure is part of the interview, creating an opportunity for the search committee to learn about the candidates, but also for candidates to learn about the institution and the position.

Among all these milestones, there are contacts between the candidate and some key participants (the search committee, the appointing officer, the search consultant). Chapter 5 takes up the nature of these contacts and what candidates can expect from each of them.

The candidate who gets the offer is the subject of Chapter 6. This is a critical moment; some candidates are so delighted to have come through the search process victorious that they immediately accept whatever is offered. Others are more ambivalent, or have more than one offer to consider. This chapter suggests items to consider as you decide whether or not to accept.

Not everyone will get the offer. Chapter 7 takes up the issues on the minds of those who are unsuccessful in the search process. What went wrong? How can you do better next time? How should you talk about the search with your references and other friends and colleagues?

Finally, the successful candidate should consider how best to make the transition into his or her new role. Chapter 8 discusses the many details that need to be taken care of (conversations with colleagues, press release and announcements on the new campus, decisions that need to be made early in the new job).

Part II: Advice for Search Committees

In Part II, the focus shifts to search committees, again moving chronologically through the search process. Chapter 9 addresses the foundational work that a search committee should do: analyzing the reason for the vacancy and the attractiveness of the position to the kinds of candidates being sought. It is important to be brutally honest in this analysis; striving for candidates who are unlikely to be interested in the position wastes time and resources and invites disappointment and a frustrated committee.

Assembling the search committee and identifying the committee chair is the subject of Chapter 10. A good search requires a good committee; attracting the best candidates is more likely if the committee is welcoming and works effectively as a team, shares the vision of the board or the president, and is well informed about the institution and the position.

Chapter 11 explains what search consultants do. If your institution is thinking about appointing a search consultant, you should consider the full range of services that can be provided and the cost. If you decide to get consulting support, you will want to select the right consultant for the project. This chapter includes advice on these issues.

Chapters 12, 13, and 14 analyze the sequence of steps in the typical search process and describe how to approach them: preparing for the search, recruiting candidates, and evaluating candidates and selecting finalists. These chapters provide essential information for institutions that decide to carry out an executive search without a consultant, but will be helpful for those working with consultants as well.

Chapter 15 takes up the process of creating a smooth transition. The campus needs to be prepared for the new president, and the new president will need to be prepared to play a new role.

Readers are encouraged to focus initially on Part I or Part II, depending on their current situation. But it is not uncommon for search committee members to become candidates soon after the search. In almost every search, someone approaches the consultant afterward to say, "Could I talk with you privately?" and the agenda is usually their own potential job search. Sometimes the person selected in the search brings a new approach that leads others to decide to move on. Sometimes committee members realize as they interview candidates that they themselves have the ability to do the job as well as or better than those being interviewed.

And candidates in one search often find themselves committee members in another. Both successful and unsuccessful candidates can make a valuable contribution to a search committee as a result of their own search experience.

For readers in all these situations, my intention is to offer concrete advice that can guide decision making, assist in sorting out complex issues, and generally enhance the process of participating in an executive search.

ACKNOWLEDGMENTS

I n 10 years as a consultant, I have worked with many wonderful people who have influenced my thinking and my work and been a source of valued colleagueship. I want to thank my colleagues at the three firms at which I have worked—Barnes and Roche, A.T. Kearney Executive Search, and Witt/Kieffer; the many clients who have trusted me to support the development of their senior leadership teams; and the hundreds of candidates I have worked with—some of whom were appointed through my searches and some not, but many of whom became clients and friends. Special thanks to Sara Angeletti, Bob Atwell, Dennis Barden, Manny Berger, Chuck Bunting, Ray Cotton, Madeleine Green, Jan Greenwood, Ann Die Hasselmo, Donna Janulis, Bruce Johnstone, Lucie Lapovsky, Nancy Archer Martin, George Mehaffy, Ilene Nagel, Susan Nalepa, Alberto Pimentel, Gary Posner, Marlene Ross, Martha Schlager, and Shelly Storbeck. Many people helped me to gather the information that I hope will make this book a useful resource for readers, including Chris Bitting, Jo Hern Curris, Zaneeta Daver, Peter Eckel, Rich Ekman, Rosemary Lauth, Dan Levin, Donna Phillips, Amy Schoeny, and Joe Zolner. Liz McMillen and Denise Magner at the *Chronicle of Higher Education*, editors of the "Moving Up" column that I wrote from 1999 to 2005, helped me to conjure up interesting column ideas and pressed me to answer the questions that readers would have; writing the column put me on the path to writing this book. Karl Amatneek, Bob Atwell, Peter Donaldson, George Dowdall, Matthew McClain, and Shelly Storbeck, among my most trusted friends, family members, and colleagues, read drafts of this manuscript and offered valuable comments, as did my editor, Susan Slesinger. My appreciation to all of them.

PART I

ADVICE FOR CANDIDATES

CHAPTER 1

Before You Start Looking

Many people aspire to lead a college or university, but the threshold—the search process—can be high, and crossing that threshold can be complicated, difficult, and protracted, as well as exhilarating and rewarding. Those aspiring to presidencies and vice presidencies are eager for the chance to articulate a vision for an institution, to persuade others to contribute the resources that enable the vision to be fulfilled, and to work with colleagues to implement the vision. The process by which an institution selects its leadership entails a series of conversations, both structured and informal, with the institution's leaders, almost always organized into search committees. In these conversations, you, as the candidate, must persuade the committee (or, in some cases, the committee must persuade you) that you are the best person for the job—as well as assuring yourself that this is the best job for you at this time.

Before becoming candidates, aspiring senior leaders prepare themselves in a variety of ways. They may serve in an administrative "gateway" position that provides essential experience, such as dean or associate vice president; participate in a professional development program, such as the Fellows Program run by the American Council on Education (ACE) or the Harvard Graduate School of Education (see Appendix A for a list of some professional development programs); and do some serious reflection to determine that they have the intellectual and psychological inclination and a record of some success at lower levels of administration. While some new presidents and vice presidents simply find themselves in these positions without having anticipated a leadership role, most today have consciously prepared for or at least considered taking this step.

WHEN TO BEGIN YOUR SEARCH

As you reflect on whether it is time to start looking for a presidency or a vice presidency, there are several important timing considerations:

Your Own Professional Readiness

Some prospective senior leaders are highly motivated to seek a new position and have a strong sense of readiness to move up in the organizational hierarchy. They want to paint on a larger canvas—addressing broader institutional issues and participating in regional or national or international leadership of higher education. They want to control more of the context that, in more limited roles, is controlled by others. Without this eagerness to lead at the next level, you probably should not pursue those positions; the jobs are too difficult to be done by someone who is not eager to do them.

The most important aspect of readiness is professional experience. The particular experience required for each position in each institution will differ somewhat, but there are some core elements. Candidates should be able to show experience in areas such as:

- *Fund-raising:* The president's most critical responsibility is to assemble the resources necessary for the institution to carry out its mission. Thus, it is essential for presidential candidates to have had some fund-raising experience. Fund-raising from individual donors is highly valued, as is working with legislators and foundations. Candidates with no fund-raising experience are at a disadvantage in presidential searches.

- *Vision:* The president—sometimes alone and sometimes in a collaborative process—establishes the institution's vision for the future. Vice presidents may be expected to articulate a vision for their areas of responsibility, and to work with the president to shape the institution-wide vision.

- *Management:* There are some successful presidents and vice presidents who had no previous management experience, but most candidates for these positions are expected to have successfully carried out basic management responsibilities such as planning, budgeting, supervising, delegating, and general problem-solving.

- *Communication and collaboration:* The culture of governance in higher education calls for considerable communication and collaboration. Vice presidents must communicate effectively with those in their areas and must collaborate with the other vice presidents. The president must communicate effectively with many internal and external audiences, and most especially must collaborate with the board of trustees.

There are two broad schools of thought on the question of experience. Most would argue that experience is essential. It provides the concrete knowledge of how things are done (how money is raised from individual donors, how curriculum revisions are undertaken, how institutional priorities are established). It provides a track record of demonstrated success—e.g., you have actually asked someone for money and perhaps they have even responded with a contribution; you have participated in curriculum development and learned how to navigate its intellectual and political complexities; you have played a major role in a strategic planning process. A record of experience in these areas gives the search committee confidence that you can do these things again in a new position with a good likelihood of success.

But there are others who argue that experience is not so important. They might say that a smart person with the right leadership instincts and good professional judgment can figure out how to do the job and, with a little support (a capable team, an effective board), can do it well. This view of leadership is most often seen in elite institutions in which scholarly accomplishment and stature are especially highly valued. In other institutions, it is rare to see search committees ready to take what they perceive to be a risk on someone who is inexperienced or untested.

As you consider entering a search process for a presidency or vice presidency, make an appraisal of your professional readiness, considering whether you are appropriately prepared for the position and the institution in which you are interested.

Personal Issues

Candidates for executive positions, like everyone else, have a variety of demands in their personal lives that require attention and compete with executive positions for their time and attention. Most of us can not do everything at once. Children have the normal needs of growing up, or may have special needs. Spouses or partners may or may not be movable for personal or professional reasons, and in addition, they may be more or less inclined to be the partner of a president. Aging parents may require attention. And your own age can be an issue, either in your own eyes, if you feel yourself starting to run out of steam, or in the eyes of a search committee, whose members may perceive that you lack the energy, the fresh ideas, or the time to stay in the job long enough. As a reference point, *The American College President* reports that in 2001, presidents appointed since 1999 had a median age of 55.[1]

Length of Service in Your Current Position

Some candidates think about length of service in terms of how soon they can leave. In general, you should not stay in a position for less than three years. And if you have left one position after a short stay, be sure not to leave the next position too quickly. You do not want to be seen as someone who hops from job to job; committees will speculate that you were fired or were not able to get along, or that you run from problems or move before really accomplishing anything.

But there is also the question of staying too long. Staying for 10 or 15 years may not be viewed by search committees as a problem, but candidates who have been in one institution for 20 or more years, particularly if this is the only institution for which they have ever worked, are often viewed with some consternation by search committees. Committee members will speculate about why someone stayed so long: Did they lack the drive to move up, or to move on to the challenges of a new environment? Do they only know one way of doing things, which they would impose on us? These questions may have good answers, but there is the risk that a committee will put your file aside before hearing your views.

Forces Propelling You to Look Elsewhere

When a new president arrives, vice presidents often leave. When there is substantial change in the membership or leadership of the board, presidents may move on. This changing institutional context may propel you to seek a new position, either because there is a lack of fit with the new person to whom you report, because the new person wants to build a new leadership team, or because you are associated with a previous conflict or the existing way of doing things and thus may be seen as a barrier to establishing a new approach. This pattern of turnover following a presidential appointment is widely understood, and in fact institutions that have had a major leadership change are prime recruiting territory for search consultants.

Sometimes the forces propelling you to look elsewhere are less benign. You may have had a serious conflict of personality or of approach with your supervisor or someone else in a key position. Your work may have been evaluated negatively and you may have been encouraged to move on, or you may simply have been fired. The situation surrounding your departure may be handled discreetly, or there may be considerable public controversy and turmoil. These situations are difficult to handle on a personal level; they should certainly cause you to make a careful evaluation of the quality of your work and how you may have contributed to the problem. But from the perspective of participating in a search process, the management of an unhappy and premature departure is difficult.

Your first hope should be that the controversy was not reported in the press or commented upon in blogs. Search engines will make these reports available to search committees indefinitely, and in spite of the fact that they may not be accurate, or may omit an ultimate resolution in your favor, they can easily harm you. The passage of time may make these reports less relevant, but it is hard to make them go away.

How can you deal with this kind of problem? You can provide a convincing understanding of the situation in your own communication with a search committee. It has to be clear and coherent, it should be presented without emotion, and it should avoid placing blame on everyone but yourself. These guidelines will not fit every situation, but they are worth keeping in mind as you reflect on how to approach your application letter or your conversation with the search consultant or the search committee. Most important of all, be sure that the committee hears about this problem from you first, and not from someone else. Your candor in coming forward will be viewed positively, even if there is concern about the problem itself; conversely, your silence on such an issue is likely to be seen as a character flaw.

Another way to deal with a problem of past performance or conflicts is to identify others who can provide the search committee with an objective appraisal of the situation and your role in it. If the troubles are widely known and are likely to be known to the committee before they get to know you, you may want this observer to send a letter of nomination on your behalf that seeks to neutralize the problem. Or, if the troubles have not been publicized and are not likely to be known to the committee until later, you can have these people provide references for you at a later stage.

Compelling Opportunities

There are many people who are thriving in their current positions and certainly are not looking for new ones, but who are captivated by a particular opportunity. Your alma mater may recruit you to be president. A position may come open near your hometown, or your new grandchild, or the city where your partner works. The compensation package offered can be so significant that it cannot be ignored. When this happens, only you can decide how to weigh the value of the opportunity against the attraction of your current situation. I would only caution you to think carefully about whether this is truly a one-time-only opportunity, or one that will come around again in the same form or a better form, when the timing may be better for your personal situation.

Quitting Your Job While You Look for a Job

Looking for a senior position can be very demanding—almost a full-time job in itself. Your written materials should be modified for each search, and if they are convincing, you will be invited for interviews that can last up to two days, plus travel time. Questions will be asked about your absence from campus, and you may find it difficult to keep up with your normal responsibilities. To accommodate these time demands, some people step down from their positions when they begin to look for presidencies or vice presidencies. Others, when they notify the board chair or president of their interest in seeking a new opportunity, are asked to step down soon, rather than waiting until a new position has been secured. If possible, avoid doing this. Obviously, stepping down entails the risk that you will find yourself with no position. But it also is likely to raise concerns in the minds of search committee members as to whether you have actually been terminated.

PURSUING OPPORTUNITIES

Once you have decided that you are ready to make a move to a presidency or a vice presidency, how do you learn about opportunities, and how do you decide which ones to pursue? In higher education, virtually all senior positions are nationally advertised, and most of them are advertised in the *Chronicle of Higher Education*. Other print and online publications are available as well. You should read them carefully to get a sense of whether you have the necessary qualifications.

If you do not have the qualifications, you should analyze the requirements, determine which experiences you are missing, and make a plan to get those experiences so that, some years from now, you can revisit the ads and be better prepared to compete for the position. If you want to be a chief academic officer and have never been a line officer to whom faculty report, you probably need to serve as a department chair or a dean. If you want to be a chief advancement officer but have only been a major gifts officer, you need to get the experience of supervising staff and directing a program within the advancement area before you can move to the top position. Presidents used to come directly from the faculty, but today are more likely to have been deans or vice presidents before moving into the presidency; spending time in those roles is not only a formal prerequisite—it also provides the very valuable opportunity to learn how to assemble a leadership team, to raise money, to articulate and implement a vision, and much more.

In my experience as a search consultant, from one-half to two-thirds of the candidates in any given search are totally unqualified for the positions for which they have applied. You do not want to be part of that group. Examine your qualifications with care and do not pursue jobs for which you have no chance of success. This is especially true if a search committee is working with a consultant. Consultants will remember that you applied for positions for which you were unqualified and they will doubt your credibility the next time, even though you might be a better fit then.

How do you know where you will be seen as a good fit and have a chance of success as a candidate? Committees typically look for candidates who have experience with similar responsibilities in similar types of institutions. If you are in a research university, you are less likely to be a convincing candidate in a community college than someone from a community college would be—and vice versa; committees will wonder whether you really grasp and value the mission and character of their institution. If you are in a nonselective public regional comprehensive master's university, you are likely to be a less convincing candidate for an elite baccalaureate institution than someone from another elite institution would be. The bigger the gap between your type of institution and the institution where the position is located, the less likely that the committee will see you as a plausible candidate. The exception to this general rule is that most institutions are eager to attract candidates from more prominent and successful institutions. Regional or nonselective institutions often seek to recruit candidates from elite institutions, but differences in institutional resources or compensation packages between these types of institutions can sometimes be barriers to the actual appointment, as candidates realize that stepping up organizationally requires some sacrifices in earning power or in the tools available to help the institution achieve its goals.

Another element that can have an impact on perception of fit is a disciplinary link or other area of professional expertise. Someone with particular disciplinary expertise (e.g., nursing, engineering, international relations) might be seen as too narrow in an institution where those fields are not prominent, but is more likely to be seen as a good fit in an institution that has particular strength in that academic area. For example, a dean of engineering is more likely to be an attractive candidate for provost or president at an institution with a strong engineering school, and a former ambassador is more likely to be an attractive candidate for provost or president at an institution that emphasizes international relations. The attractiveness of certain kinds of professional expertise can also help a candidate to overcome a search committee's initially narrow expectations; for example, an institution might be seeking a president with a traditional academic background, but its strong need for philanthropic contributions might create a preference for a candidate who is an advancement professional, or its financial challenges might create a preference for a candidate who is a chief financial officer.

Some candidates, often described as "nontraditional," come from outside higher education—e.g., from leadership roles in public service, in law firms or in other nonprofit organizations. Search committees often ask to see nontraditional candidates in the pool, perhaps because trustees (who typically come from the corporate world) expect to have an affinity for candidates from the corporate sector, and that candidates with this background will have a better approach to institutional leadership. However, even search committees that express an initial interest in nontraditional candidates more often select the traditional candidates who have backgrounds in higher education.

To be successful as a candidate, individuals from outside the academy should consider whether they can make a convincing case that they understand the issues and the culture of higher education. When I talk with individuals seeking to move into higher education, I encourage them to develop expertise by becoming trustees, getting involved with fund-raising for their alma mater, teaching courses or even giving guest lectures—and thus building familiarity and relationships and potentially getting to know individuals in higher education who can serve as references. These kinds of experiences can help candidates to evaluate their interest and to convince a search committee that they would be a good fit.

INTERNAL CANDIDATES

One of the most complicated search situations is that of internal candidates who pursue positions at their current institutions. There is no doubt that internal candidates are placed under a microscope during the search process. They are better known to colleagues on the search committee than are the other candidates, for better or worse—internal candidates may have some strong supporters on the committee, as well as implacable opposition. There may be political considerations outside the committee that have an impact on the appointment. The application letter will be scrutinized for accuracy in representation of accomplishments; candidates who say, for example, "I led the institutional accreditation process," may be challenged by committee members who think that someone else actually provided the leadership while the candidate was only the figurehead or only the supporting staff member, or who think that the candidate did lead the process—but did a terrible job.

Sometimes internal candidates see themselves as the heir apparent, and their colleagues may encourage them to see themselves in this way. If you are the successful vice president for advancement in an institution that desperately needs more private philanthropy, and you are known and loved by all the alumni, how could the board not select you to be president? But boards may have other issues in mind—the need for new blood and the new ideas of a (possibly younger) outsider, the need for someone with impeccable academic credentials, and so on. Resist being seduced by the assumption that the position is yours, no matter how many people assure you of this. There are virtually no guarantees.

The situation for an internal candidate is especially thorny when he or she holds the interim position. A dean, for example, may be asked to serve as interim provost, and simultaneously is a candidate for the permanent appointment. This can be like having a yearlong interview. Should you make significant institutional decisions and thus commit your successor to directions that may not make sense to him or her? Should you take bold stands to show your true colors, and risk alienating key decision makers? Should you play things safe to avoid making enemies, but thereby take the risk of being seen as weak and indecisive? Every day may seem to provide opportunities to win or lose votes on the committee. Most people who have successfully navigated these waters say that you can only do the job in the way you think best; if the committee does not support the approach you take, you would not be a good fit for the position anyway.

Assuming you do wish to be a candidate for the permanent position, there is the question of whether and when to apply. You have a wide range of options —you can apply early, or at the last minute, or not at all (instead waiting for the committee to approach you). You can keep your candidacy confidential, you can respond to questions about your candidacy if you are asked, or you can actively lobby for the support of your colleagues. You can be a candidate eagerly or reluctantly, showing enthusiasm for the opportunity to lead, or conveying the reservations that you have as a result of the nature of the position or the resources allocated to it or your personal situation (e.g., the need to give attention at this time to aging parents, young children, a new marriage, or a dissolving relationship). Obviously you will need to make your own choices based on the particulars of the situation and your own best judgment. Let me offer just a few words of guidance for internal candidates.

Do Not Lobby

If your friends and colleagues spontaneously convey their enthusiasm to the committee, you may even want to consider reining them in, or at least expressing your reservations. The hazard is that the committee will perceive that you have encouraged them to lobby on your behalf. I have seen candidates who lobby nationally, letting their colleagues at other institutions know that they are candidates—or even saying that they are guaranteed to get the position and, as a result, discouraging others who might apply. If this gets back to the committee, it is viewed with great alarm and does not serve you well.

Consider What Risks You Want to Take

If you apply as an internal candidate, there is some chance that you will be selected. But knowing that you might not be selected, what risks are you taking by applying? Many potential internal candidates fear that, if they are not selected for the position, they will have to leave the institution. They speculate that the new person may see them as a previous competitor with a base of support that could be mobilized, or simply someone too closely associated with the previous administration. Of course, the new person may hold this view of you even if you are not a candidate. Many unsuccessful internal candidates become successful partners of the candidate who is selected, so I would encourage you to not to assume that you will have to leave if you are not selected.

There are also risks to your candidacy at other institutions; if you apply and are not selected, you will be asked to account for this when you enter subsequent searches at other institutions. On the other hand, if you decide not to apply, but search committees elsewhere are aware of the search at your institution, you will probably be asked to account for why you were not a candidate. With regard to subsequent searches, there are risks no matter what you do.

If you do decide to apply, there is also the question of how and when to do that. Some candidates apply because they think they have the needed skills and experiences and want to do the job. Others await a signal from the search committee that their candidacy will receive a favorable response. Waiting for such a signal can save you from the wasted effort and embarrassment of an unsuccessful candidacy, but there is always the chance that the committee is not inclined to show its preferences and is waiting instead for you to step forward and show your interest. So, waiting for a sign offers some security, but also some risk.

Formulate a Clear and Consistent Message for Your Colleagues

You can be sure that your colleagues will be gossiping about your potential candidacy. Formulate the message you want to convey, and try to convey it consistently. For example, "Yes, I am going to be a candidate, but my hope is that we will select the best possible CFO. If I am not selected, I will look forward to working with the person who is selected." Or, "Yes, I am going to be a candidate, and I stand for a particular vision for the future of this institution. If that vision is not supported by the board of trustees, then I will feel that it is best to move on to another institution where my views will be better received."

DIVERSITY CANDIDATES

Candidates who are in some significant way different from the group that dominates the institution and its leadership face some special issues in senior searches. I am referring here especially to women candidates for positions in institutions whose president and vice presidents are all men, and to people of color who are candidates in majority institutions, but other candidates who are different from the group that dominates the institution should consider these issues as well. Some women and people of color move easily and quickly up the administrative ranks and into presidencies, but others find the process especially frustrating and difficult to navigate.

The critical decision is which searches to enter. Some women and people of color decide not to enter searches at institutions in which underrepresentation leads them to believe the institution is inhospitable to diversity. Some look for information about how the institution has dealt with issues of racism or sexual harassment. Some seek information about women and people of color who held leadership roles in the past and try to learn whether they found a supportive environment, hospitable to diverse leaders and conducive to their success. The conclusions that candidates draw can lead them to decide whether or not to enter the search. This is a reasonable approach, but prospective candidates should also consider whether an institution with a poor record on these factors is striving to change and is capable of changing, and whether they are willing and able to play a role in shaping a new diversity identity for the institution.

Entering searches repeatedly but not being selected is a painful experience. It can be extremely disturbing to be recruited repeatedly for presidential or vice presidential searches, to be interviewed, to become a finalist, and then not to be selected. Candidates wonder whether they are being used as window dressing, as a token woman or person of color (or both) to round out an otherwise white and/or male slate of candidates, creating the appearance of diversity in the candidate pool even though the diversity candidate really never has a chance of selection. There is no doubt that this situation occurs. Some diversity candidates are drawn into searches because they bring diversity, and not because they genuinely have an opportunity to be selected. Having said that, it must also be said that if they do not participate in the search, they will not be selected either. The candidate's very difficult job is to decide whether the chances of selection are great enough to justify the price of participating in the search.

My advice is to take a few risks in entering even some searches that appear to be inhospitable, and to use those searches as opportunities to strengthen your presentation of yourself both on paper and in person. Learn as much as you can about how you are doing, how you can do better, and where your candidacy will be viewed most positively. Do as much as you can to strengthen your skills and experience in your current position so that you have more to offer as a candidate. Consider how best to talk with search committees, presidents, and boards about issues of gender and ethnicity.

Having decided which searches to enter, women and people of color, like all candidates, have to be as effective as possible in presenting themselves, and probably they have to be even better than others. As long as boards are dominated by white men, and presidents are more likely to be white men than to be women or people of color, the inclination to select candidates who resemble oneself will create a bias toward selecting other white men. A candidate seeking to overcome this bias seems to require an extra measure of accomplishment or impressiveness. Until that bias is removed, the challenges for diversity candidates will continue.

NOTES

1. Melanie E. Corrigan, *The American College President* (Washington, DC: American Council on Education, 2002), 102.

CHAPTER 2

Preparing Your Application

O nce you have decided to be a candidate, you have a critical opportunity to present yourself both persuasively and accurately to the search committee. As a search consultant, when I am trying to recruit highly desirable candidates, I sometimes tell them that the process is really very simple, but I know that this is not completely true; the process, done right, is demanding. In this chapter, I will describe the concrete steps of preparing your materials; these materials give the committee its first glimpse of you and can make or break your candidacy. If you are dropped as a candidate at this stage, you are unlikely to be reactivated—it is all over for this particular search. If you want this position, you need to invest time, thought, and effort in preparing your materials, which will normally include your cover letter, curriculum vitae, list of references, and other items the committee may request. The most important piece of advice I can offer is that candidates whose materials reflect an understanding of the institution make a far stronger first impression than candidates whose materials appear to the committee to be generic, or—even worse—whose materials appear to be intended for a different search!

GATHERING INFORMATION ABOUT THE INSTITUTION AND THE POSITION

Before you prepare your materials, do some research about the institution and the position. One of the burdens of the Web is that you have to use it. There is no excuse for not having reviewed the institutional Web site with some care. In addition to that site, you should use all the other search tools that are available, such as Google, newspaper databases, Guidestar.com for institutional tax forms and other data, the *Chronicle of Higher Education* and other higher-education publications, and the annual reports of *U.S. News and World Report*. As you review these sites, you can almost always learn a great deal about an organization's structure; its mission, vision, and strategic planning; and its recent accomplishments—and sometimes much more.

Use your personal network, too. If you know people who can give you critical insights about the institution and the position that will not be on the Web, and you are willing to let these people know that you have an interest in the position, call them and ask them some key questions. Why did the previous president or vice president leave? What are the current institutional issues—resources, enrollment, student quality, rankings, accreditation, relations with the surrounding community or with the legislature, etc.? What is the campus climate, and how is morale? Are students pleased with their educational experience? Knowledge of these issues can help you make better decisions about whether you are interested in the position, and can help you shape your materials more effectively. If these conversations yield confidential or controversial information (e.g., the president is about to be charged with harassment or embezzlement), do not reflect that information in your materials. Using all the available and appropriate information and any extra intelligence you have been able to gather will show the search committee that you are seriously interested in the position they are seeking to fill.

WAYS OF ENTERING A SEARCH—
APPLICATION, NOMINATION AND RECRUITMENT

Before you assemble your materials and submit them—and typically you will be submitting them electronically—consider whether you are applying following a nomination, responding to recruitment by a search consultant, or simply applying directly on your own. Each may call for a slightly different approach.

Nominations

The higher the level of the position, the greater the value of a nomination. Presidential candidates are most often nominated, and the nomination can have particular value if the nominator is known to the search committee or the consultant. As a consultant, if I know and respect the nominator, I am predisposed to take the candidate especially seriously. If the nominator phones me with an enthusiastic endorsement rather than simply sending a quick e-mail, or has sent me strong candidates in the past, or is known as a great judge of talent, I consider these elements in my appraisal of the candidate, especially of one whom I do not already know. Nominations can also be useful if you have been through rough spots in your career and need an objective observer to comment on the complexities of your situation (e.g., "You may know that Jack left his previous institution prematurely; there were many, including me, who regretted his departure, but having observed the situation, I have to say that a very contentious faculty had rejected three very capable deans in three years. His early departure does not reflect poorly on Jack—in fact, given the circumstances, he was quite a successful dean.").

Working with a Search Consultant

If consultants are involved in the search, you will normally find their contact information listed in the ad or the position specification that should be available on the institution's or the consultant's Web site. If the consultant has contacted you, you can ask in what ways you seem to be a good fit, and in what areas you may be lacking the right experience. Listen carefully to the answer. Some consultants may, as they learn more about your background, simply suggest you not invest time in this search. Others may be more circumspect, suggesting that you bring some strengths and some areas of weaker preparation, just as all candidates will. In the end, you alone must decide whether to apply.

Although some candidates may be well known to the consultant at the start of the search, either from other searches or through general professional networks, other candidates may be referred to the consultant through a nomination process. Consultants routinely contact leaders in the field (e.g., the president who heads the association of presidents in a state system of higher education, or the head of a national organization of research universities like the American Association of Universities, or of liberal arts colleges like the Council of Independent Colleges) to request their suggestions of candidates. These individuals offer the names of prospective candidates who are then contacted directly to determine their interest and suitability for the position. This process of "sourcing" is an essential element in building a candidate pool; if your name is offered by one or more of these sources, the credibility of your candidacy is enhanced.

Sometimes individuals who are themselves interested in being candidates for a position are also asked to suggest nominations of others, or may be asked by colleagues to provide a nomination or a reference. This small-world phenomenon occurs more often than one might think, and it is especially common for candidates to list as references individuals who are also candidates in the same search. (The latter can easily happen if the candidate has a group of colleagues who serve as references as needed, not requiring a request before each search; or if you as a candidate provide a reference list with the understanding that you will have the opportunity to notify your references before they are contacted by the committee or consultant.) If you are, or wish to be, a candidate, you should consider how to handle a sourcing request or a request to serve as a reference. One approach is to decline either request and keep the search committee focused on your role as a candidate, avoiding any questions about conflict of interest. Another is to serve willingly as a source or a reference in the interest of seeking the best fit for the institution's needs. Your stance in this approach would be that there may be many highly qualified candidates and the committee and board should have a range of strong prospects to choose from as they seek the one judged to have the best fit. This approach can be perceived as highly professional and reflecting well on your candidacy, even though you have supported the candidacy of others.

Applying for a Position on Your Own

There are probably many presidents and vice presidents who applied directly for their positions after reading an advertisement. If a search committee did not really wish to encourage direct applications, why would it advertise? If there is no consultant, direct application may truly be encouraged. But if there is a consultant, you may get a significantly better response to your candidacy if you are nominated or recruited. The reason for this is that the consultant is striving to present the committee with the best possible candidates, and when your name is suggested by a respected leader in higher education, the credibility of your candidacy is enhanced.

COVER LETTERS

The Ambiguities of Cover Letters

Your cover letter holds a peculiar position within your set of materials. Each committee member tends to believe that his or her own reading of your narrative gives a true window on your soul. The problem is that committee members may read your letter very differently. One person will say, "I loved this letter—it is so inspiring," while another says, "This letter was full of platitudes and generalities." Where does this leave the candidate? My advice is to focus on getting your letter to say what you want it to say, and to say it in a way that the reader will understand. If you write a broadly philosophical letter, also provide some examples to illustrate your points. If you write a very concrete letter, be sure that the breadth of your vision is also apparent. Weigh the advantages and disadvantages of different approaches before you draft and then finalize your letter.

Focus on the Institution

It is important to keep in mind that your letter should be more about the institution that is searching than it is about you. The strengths and experiences that you bring should be described in the context of what the institution is looking for. If you have had extensive experience revising the core curriculum as dean of arts and sciences, you should consider whether and how that experience is relevant to a provost position. If you are an advancement vice president who has supervised a staff of 50 professionals in a large university, consider how that experience is relevant to the presidency of a small private college. If you are a chief student affairs or enrollment officer, show how your deep understanding of student satisfaction issues will enable you to enhance student life and thus improve enrollment and increase revenue as president. Your letter should say, in essence, "From what I have been able to learn, this is what I believe University X needs in the coming years. Here are some examples of what I have done that will enable me to provide leadership for those aspects of your institution."

Sometimes search committees are very clear about what they are looking for. They may specify, for example, that their primary presidential challenges are legislative relations, building a stronger sense of campus community life, and increasing institutional stature and recognition. Candidates sometimes write letters directed precisely to this list of challenges. I think this is a good approach. If the list of expectations for the position is long, the letter can grow to become many pages of bullet points. Excessive length diminishes effectiveness. Find an approach that blends the expectations together more subtly while still touching on most of them and the strengths and experiences you would bring to each, or that focuses on a few of the key points where you can shine, perhaps alluding to the others but saving full discussion for later steps in the search process.

Although committees may be clear about what they are looking for, they are not always in full agreement. Underneath the clarity there may be layers of disparate expectations. The trustees may be seeking a fund-raiser, the faculty may be seeking an academic visionary, and the students may be seeking someone who will be accessible and visible on campus. You might use your letter to explore what you would bring to these (not always compatible) expectations.

The cover letter should tell readers something about you that goes beyond what they can learn from your CV. In your letter, do not repeat the steps in your career unless you want to make a specific point about them, e.g., "I have served in both large public research universities and selective small private colleges, and attended a church-related undergraduate college, so I am familiar with the culture of a variety of institutional environments." If campus climate is an issue at the institution you are interested in, you can use the letter to comment on how you have enhanced campus climate (something unlikely to be reflected in your CV). Be selective. You cannot write about everything, and you do not want to send a 10-page letter. But if you write a very short letter that is little more than a letter of transmittal—i.e., "Please accept my application for the presidency"—you have missed a very significant opportunity to make your case to the search committee.

Style

Avoid platitudes, especially those that may be currently in vogue. I react badly to letters that say, "I am a collaborative leader; my door is always open; I listen carefully but then I am able to make a decision," unless examples are also provided to substantiate the claims. Avoid writing a series of sentences that all begin with "I"; readers often interpret this to mean that you do not work well with others. But not everyone will agree about what makes a good letter. You should take the approach that most fully reflects your style.

Candidates Who Do Not Provide a Cover Letter

Although the cover letter can add value to your materials, there are some candidates who are not willing to provide a letter. Sometimes these are the strongest candidates. They are most often concerned about "deniability"—that is, they cannot be in a position of having actively sought the presidency of another institution, perhaps because they are currently a president and the board would be dismayed or the faculty would be gleeful if it were known they were considering making a move. Sometimes candidates are unwilling to provide a letter because of a strong sense of self-worth, believing that, if the committee knows how excellent they are as candidates, the committee will pursue them and they will not have to make the gesture of formally applying. There are even some prospective candidates who decline to provide a CV, letting the committee or the consultant know that it is available on the Web.

The dilemma for a candidate who takes this approach is that a committee may or may not be enticed into the pursuit. Some committees will view a candidate who declines to provide a letter or other basic information as arrogant, lacking in respect for the search process, or not really interested in the position, and may decide to drop your candidacy. But if a candidate is believed to be extremely strong, some committees will gladly make the effort to work around the constraints. They can use alternative methods of getting to know the candidate's views and approach, such as reading reports or speeches that the candidate has written. If you prefer not to provide a cover letter, realize that you run the risk of denying yourself the opportunity to get this position; this is especially true if there is no search consultant.

REFERENCE LISTS

Just as the cover letter reflects your identity in the context of institutional needs, your list of references reveals significant elements of who you are. Your list of references will depend of course on who can speak persuasively about you. Suggestions about whom to include on reference lists are in Appendix B.

Some candidates are reluctant to include a list of references with an initial application, fearing that the references will be contacted prematurely and that confidentiality will be breached. Some searches do not require a list of references. But in both these cases, there may be value in providing a list of references because it can add considerable strength to your candidacy. If you are able to provide an impressive list of higher education leaders who know you well and are willing to speak on your behalf, this in itself enhances your candidacy, even before the references are contacted. Not all reference lists have this quality, but if yours does, your candidacy is enhanced by including it.

THE CURRICULUM VITAE

The curriculum vitae is the heart of your identity insofar as the search committee knows you. I have left it for last in this discussion of preparing materials because it is the least variable—your career path, your publications, and your community service are what they are, and while you can show them in different ways, you have far more flexibility to shape your letter and list of references. But even your CV is not immutable; it too should be shaped with care. A few suggestions:

- *Be meticulously accurate.* Even minor inaccuracies or typographical errors can be viewed as efforts to deceive. If you are seen as lacking in integrity, nothing else will count.

- *Include an appropriate level of detail,* recognizing that the greatest risk for most candidates is including too much. Do not be the candidate who submits the 50-page résumé, particularly in a presidential search for which the search committee is likely to include board members who come from the corporate world and who are used to seeing résumés of only a page or two. What details can be dropped to shorten a long CV? You do not need to list every committee you have ever served on, or every course you have taught. Scholarly and creative work can pose a dilemma for those who have been very productive. If you list everything, your CV may run to 70 pages. Consider first the composition of the search committee and the level of the position. If the committee has many faculty members on it (which is especially likely to be the case for provost searches), they may want to see your full list of publications. If the committee includes more non-faculty, consider providing an abbreviated list; you can use a selected list that presents only the most significant publications or speeches or grants, or a list of recent publications (e.g., for the past five or 10 years). Another alternative is to place your detailed list of publications in an attachment or addendum.

- *Use a format and provide content that will be the most helpful to the reader.* By this I mean that you should use bullets to break up a narrative and make it easier to read. Use keywords to group similar items together and highlight areas of your strength (e.g., "International activities: participation in establishing my university's program in Hong Kong, supervision of the office of international students and scholars, service on the committee to increase international enrollment"), or use summary statements so that you can omit details of dates and places (e.g., "National leadership: service on the boards of three national professional associations in the last decade, including chairing the strategic planning committee and serving on the program committee for the national meeting."). Naturally you will not omit any elements that the committee is likely to want to know (e.g., what you were doing between 1997 and 1999, or whether you were ever promoted to the rank of professor).

- *The career path is the most important element of your CV.* List your current and previous positions in reverse chronological order. Include key information about your institution (e.g., enrollment), and elements of your position that are not obvious. The way you format your list of positions can be significant. For example, if you have held many different positions at a single institution, highlighting each position may make it look as though you have moved every two years. At first glance, the reader may not notice that all these two-year positions were at the same institution. In a case like this, consider making the name of the institution the prominent feature of the list, with each job title and dates underneath it. If, on the other hand, you have moved from one institution to the next at a reasonable pace, staying five or more years at each, you can organize your career steps by position, which has the effect of highlighting your movement into increasingly significant responsibilities.

Before you press the "send" key, proofread your materials with care. Check for spelling errors (especially in portions of the text that are capitalized, since spell-checking software may not screen these portions), make sure you remove any traces of the name of institutions you applied to previously, and make sure that software that you used to track changes while editing have been managed so that only the final text is visible. These materials should be your best work, standing as an example of the quality of work you would do if you were selected.

CHAPTER 3

Preliminary Interviews

Preliminary interviews are one of the most critical elements in the search process. Search committee members, like many people involved in any selection process, tend to put a great deal of faith in their ability to look others in the eye, listen to them talk, and make an accurate appraisal of their characteristics and their ability to be successful in the position. Unfortunately, few actually have the ability to predict job performance based on an interview. It is particularly striking that at the conclusion of an interview, different search committee members may have very different reactions, and it is hard to know whose prediction of a candidate's potential to succeed will turn out to be most accurate. From the candidate's perspective, the goal is to present oneself both attractively and accurately. In my experience, there are many candidates whose daily reality is different from the impressions generated in an interview, and in fact many whose job performance is better than it might appear from an interview. In this chapter, I will try to demystify the preliminary interview and to provide assistance for candidates who want to do better at conveying their best selves to the committee.

First, a word about authenticity. As much as a candidate may want the job for which he or she is interviewing, there is little to be gained by presenting yourself in a manner that does not reflect you as you really are. If you are highly energized in normal life, but discipline yourself to present a lower-key impression, or if you are normally reflective and indecisive, but present yourself in an interview as a rapid decision maker, no one is well served. The committee will be dismayed to find out later that your normal behavior is inconsistent with what they saw in the interview. Worst of all, you will be burdened with trying to be a person that you are not. My advice is not intended to encourage you to distort yourself in an interview. But doubtless you have many strengths that you want to demonstrate. And there are many foolish comments that you can and should learn to avoid making, particularly as you are creating an initial impression with a search committee. If you consider some of this advice, you will be able to show yourself both more attractively and more accurately.

WHAT ARE PRELIMINARY INTERVIEWS?

Preliminary interviews are an opportunity for committees and candidates to meet in person for an hour or two and to decide whether there is enough mutual attraction to proceed to more extensive involvement in the search. Although they are common, preliminary interviews are not a part of every search. Also known as "airport interviews" or "off-site interviews," these are meetings typically held at an off-campus location where the candidates' confidentiality can be preserved, and where transportation problems are minimized by proximity to the airport where most candidates arrive.

In addition to scheduling a meeting of the candidate with the search committee, some institutions add other elements to this event. There may be an opportunity to see the campus, either in a tour arranged by the institution, or by encouraging candidates to rent a car or take a taxi and visit the campus on their own. There may be a chance to meet the appointing officer—e.g., the president may participate in interviews for vice presidential candidates. This is an extremely valuable element of the process, particularly when candidates have only a tentative interest in the position and need to be persuaded to continue in the search. Candidates have the chance to meet the person to whom they would report and at least make an initial appraisal of the chemistry between them. Equally important, the president has the opportunity to meet and to assess the candidates. In some cases the president's reaction will be conveyed to the search committee so that candidates whom the president prefers are retained for further consideration, and so that candidates whom the president does not like are not moved through the rest of the search process when there is no real chance of ultimately being selected. If many candidates are invited to a preliminary interview, this takes a great deal of the president's time, but many presidents feel it is a good investment. As a search consultant, I strongly endorse this practice.

Why Hold a Preliminary Interview?

The second-round interview, typically on campus and involving more participants, is a major event that is demanding and time-consuming, and only a few candidates are selected to take that step. Selecting candidates for the campus interview without seeing and screening them face-to-face in advance is highly risky. Consultants typically interview candidates before discussing their credentials with a search committee, but there can be a difference between a consultant's appraisal and the committee's judgment. Early committee exposure to the candidates in a preliminary interview is a very valuable step.

What Happens in a Preliminary Interview?

Essentially, candidates talk with the search committee (and the consultant, if one is involved in the search) about the position and the expectations for candidates, answering committee questions and having the opportunity to ask questions of their own. Although some search committees take a free-form approach and treat the interview as an evolving conversation, guided perhaps only by a shared understanding of what the position requires, most committees take a more structured approach. Candidates can expect to be asked a series of questions that should bear some relationship to the position description—for example, if the new vice president for advancement will be asked to lead a capital campaign, candidates should expect to be asked about their prior campaign experience. Appendix C contains some typical interview questions.

PRELIMINARY INTERVIEWS
BY PHONE AND VIDEOCONFERENCE

Some institutions are unable to manage the cost of flying up to a dozen candidates to their area, and these committees may consider instead having screening interviews by conference call or by videoconference. I find that this form of screening is considerably more inaccurate from a committee's perspective, and considerably more difficult for candidates, than the in-person preliminary interview.

Conference calls leave the candidate stranded without any visual cues. The candidate, who cannot see the committee, risks talking over someone in the meeting room. The eye contact that contributes to building a sense of connection is missing. If reception is bad, the candidate may not really be able to hear the questions; asking to have the question repeated is entirely appropriate, and much better than answering the wrong question, but it keeps the conversation from flowing naturally. The challenge to the candidate is to listen very carefully, trying quickly to recognize voices and the name of the person speaking. The greatest hazard is talking too long; I have no data on this, but it is my strong impression that a comment of a given length is perceived to be longer when it is coming over a speakerphone than when it comes from someone in the same room, and the audience loses interest more quickly.

Videoconference interviews are more effective from both the committee's and the candidate's perspective than phone interviews, but they are still substantially less effective than interviews in person. Typically, candidates will go to a commercial location where video equipment is available, and the interview follows the same procedures as the in-person interview. There may be an annoying time lag that causes the people at opposite ends of the video connection to speak over each other. Although there will be some visual cues, the picture may not be sharp enough to allow the candidate to see which committee member is smiling and which is scowling or nodding off. My impression is that video flattens the demeanor of a candidate; people with normally exuberant personalities appear less dynamic on video, and people of reserved demeanor may appear extremely flat or bland.

PREPARING FOR INTERVIEWS
Learning about the Institution

Careful preparation for interviews at every stage of the search process is essential, extending the work that you did before you assembled your written materials. You will be judged in part by how well prepared you are. You must review the material written for the search, describing the position and the institution. If this has not been sent to you, it is typically available on the institution's or the consultant's Web site. You should also review the rest of the institutional Web site, focusing on the basic demographics (size, organizational structure, budget), the major processes that may be underway (regional accreditation review, capital campaign, construction of new residence halls, strategic planning process, etc.), the campus culture (difficult to discern, but sometimes revealed in press releases and other featured elements on the site, and something that campus colleagues may be able to discuss with you), and current issues (revealed perhaps in the minutes of the university senate, which are often available on a site with some digging). You may have been sent a package of materials about the institution, and of course you should review these with care. You may not be able to get a full command of the materials, but note the salient or distinctive points so that you can comment on them during your conversation, so that you can ask about them during the interview, and so that you can respond to questions about them from the committee.

Some candidates like to do a Web search on all the committee members. Normally you will know who these people are, either because names are posted on the Web, or because they have been sent to you in advance of the interview. Gathering this information is generally a good idea, as long as it is not overdone. I remember a candidate who said to a committee member, "I see you went to Camp Lakeside when you were 10." The committee member was taken aback, and not pleased. On the other hand, offering congratulations on a recent award, or expressing interest in a research area, can be appropriate in moderation. When used to excess, this often looks to the committee like pandering.

Coaching and Practicing

There are many other ways to prepare for a preliminary interview, including reviewing lists of questions that you might get in a typical interview (see Appendix C). You can do this alone or you can find a colleague to work with you, functioning as a kind of coach. An honest coach is probably the best resource you can have, but such a person is not easy to find. Think hard about who can best play this role, seeking someone who will be honest and not simply say, "Gee, that was great. I can't think of anything that would improve it." Your coach can help you with both content and style. In terms of content, he or she can help to formulate practice questions, going through the job description and making up a few questions about each item, which you can then answer. Your coach can help you to think about some generic questions that you are likely to be asked—for instance, "Tell us about the least successful decision you have made, and what you learned from dealing with the fallout." You can work on responding to questions in areas in which you are less well prepared. Say you are a provost or a vice president for student affairs seeking a presidency, and you have had no experience with fund-raising. How will you deal with a question about your readiness to raise millions of dollars from private donors? I am not advocating preparing written answers. But I am advocating preparation so that, when predictable questions are asked in the interview, you will not be grasping for thoughts and words. The more emotionally charged the question is for you personally, the more likely that your spontaneous answer will not be your best answer. Preparation is enormously valuable.

Preparing for Difficult Questions

Preparing for difficult questions sometimes means talking about difficult periods in your career—votes of no confidence, press reports that questioned your integrity or effectiveness, premature departures from a position, and so on. Some committees may be reluctant to generate conflict in an interview by asking about these things, but most do want to learn about them. A committee that is unaware of these difficulties may learn about them later and wonder in retrospect why they never came up in the interview. A candidate should reflect with care about what to say (especially if not asked directly), and how to say it. A general principle is that a committee that hears bad news from the candidate is likely to be more tolerant of it than a committee that hears the bad news from someone else (e.g., by searching the Web, or by talking with references). If you reveal the information yourself, or if you answer questions with candor, you will at least be viewed as forthcoming. From your perspective as a candidate, you have the opportunity to tell the story in your own terms. A second principle, suggested by one of my colleagues, is to tell the story in a way that provides the essential information and then gets the topic off the table. There are always long versions and short versions, one-sided versions and broader perspectives, emotional versions and objective versions, self-enhancing and self-denigrating versions, etc. Consider all these perspectives on your story as you plan and rehearse how to tell it. Practice telling it so that you are comfortable with it and so that, under the stress of an interview, you do not inadvertently drift into a version of the story that you do not wish to tell.

Avoiding Answers That Are Too Long or Too Short

Some candidates are inclined to give short answers and others to provide longer commentaries. In higher education searches, there seems to me to be a greater inclination toward overly long answers. If this is the hazard that you personally face, work on monitoring your responses. Try to focus your thoughts before you begin to talk so that you know the three points you want to make. Make those points, offer examples, and stop. If you are inclined to repeat yourself or to ramble onto other themes, sometimes even forgetting the question to which you are responding, practice monitoring your comments and disciplining yourself to stay on point. But do not go so far toward conciseness that you omit examples. Examples, especially if they are presented with the appropriate amount of detail, can be the most convincing element of your presentation.

If, on the other hand, your hazard is offering overly short answers, try to learn not only to answer the overtly asked question, but also to respond to the broader interest that lies behind the question. For example, if you are asked, "Have you played a leadership role in providing vision for your institution?" you will want to say more than "Yes," and you will want to say something other than "Well, I am only a vice president, and the president provides that leadership." A better answer might be, "Naturally the president provides the institutional leadership (which is why I am seeking the presidency of your institution), but I have provided leadership for my division, both internally and in building partnerships with the other divisions. Let me give you a couple of examples..."

Candidate Questions for the Search Committee

Preparation for asking your own questions is just as important as preparing to answer the committee's questions. Normally you will be given an opportunity as part of your interview to ask questions of the committee, and failing to have several substantial questions is a huge missed opportunity. You miss the chance to learn something that you need to know. But you also miss the opportunity to show the committee that you take this conversation seriously and have thought about the position and its institutional context. Many candidates ask something fairly generic, such as "What is the committee really looking for in the next president?" While this may seem like a good question, you should already have some sense of the answer. This question (which I confess to having asked in some of my own less successful candidacies) shows no particular insight on your part. There are better variants on this question (e.g., "Can you tell me about the range of expectations for this position; for instance, to what degree might the faculty and the board have different perspectives on what they are looking for in the next president?" Or, "How might the science faculty and the humanities faculty differ in their hopes for the new provost?")

Other good questions show that you have been listening to the questions you were asked. The candidate might say, "I noticed that when we were talking about expectations for tenure, some people seemed to think the expectations were quite clear, but others found them mysterious. Can you tell me more about how the deans have conveyed expectations to junior faculty?"

Questions can try to get beneath the surface of the institution. You might ask, for example, about the students and why they attend—or why some drop out—what the student culture is like, or how the admission office shapes the entering class. You might ask about morale and what are the burning issues of the day.

Whatever you decide to ask, remember that you are being judged by the quality of your questions and plan them accordingly. And remember to listen to the answers and engage committee members in a conversation; instead of using the committee's answer as a launching pad to say more about yourself, use their comments to learn more about the institution and to show how interested you are in the position.

Beginning and Ending

In every interview, there are two guaranteed moments—the beginning, and the end. Prepare for both of them. Think in advance about what you'd like to say at the start, preferably something positive (e.g., thanking the committee for the invitation, rather than offering a gratuitous complaint about the traffic or the service in the hotel). At the end, when you may feel some relief that the interview is over, you will be better off if you have thought in advance about the last message you want to give to the committee, including your thanks. In the absence of prepared comments, some candidates will say "That wasn't as bad as I expected," which does not convey the impression of confidence that you want to give. A better closing might include thanks for the invitation to interview and some positive comments about the position or the search committee. Ideally these comments will be sincerely meant but, even if it has been an uncongenial group, politeness at this moment is more important than sincerity.

ELEMENTS OF STYLE

Sometimes style trumps substance. Even the best answers—the most thoughtful, well-organized, and insightful—can be poorly received if they are delivered in a lackluster fashion, in a hostile tone, or in an excessively manic style. As I have said, candidates who are normally subdued or sardonic or dynamic should present themselves as they are, seeking a committee and an institution that will resonate with this style. But there are many candidates who are engaging and good humored in normal life, but become flat or edgy because of the anxiety of an interview. Your coach may be able to give you feedback about this, or you may sense it yourself. I suspect that the best strategy for this situation is practice. Some of your practice can be "off stage," but some may come in interviews in which you make an effort to act more like your normal self and gradually achieve that goal. If you are invited to many airport interviews because of your strong credentials, but never go beyond this stage of the selection process, the style that you demonstrate may be something to which you need to give substantial attention.

Another stylistic element that can shape the committee's response to you is appearance, including clothing, jewelry, and makeup. Wearing a lot of jewelry may be more appropriate in some parts of the country than others (compare, for example, Los Angeles and rural Wisconsin). Wearing heavy scents can be both distracting and allergy-provoking. Most candidates want to be more memorable for what they say than for what they wear, so I would encourage dressing conservatively, typically both men and women wearing suits. The candidate who wears striking jewelry, cowboy boots at an interview in the northeast, or scarves that keep sliding out of place while you are talking, distracts the search committee from listening to what he or she is saying. But having said this, I have to admit that one of the most extraordinarily successful candidates I have ever seen came to her interview in a bright red suit that helped her to light up the room and to create a powerful and distinctive image for the committee. The preliminary interview is a perfect opportunity to get a haircut or buy a new suit. If you need to lose weight, this is the time to do it.

Every committee member brings a slightly different frame of reference and preferences to the interview and to the evaluation of candidates. But committee members all want to look you in the eye and seem to believe that doing so provides a window on your true identity. I mean "look you in the eye" quite literally. Eye contact is invariably an element of committee response to candidates. Candidates who look over the heads of committee members, who look directly at the men but not the women or vice versa, who seem to speak only to the most powerful people in the room (e.g., the committee chair, the trustees), who ignore the students on the committee—these candidates can expect to be criticized for this. Monitor your behavior so that this does not happen. Practice making eye contact and get in the habit of doing this. You may find this uncomfortable at first, but it is worth the effort. There are other elements of body language that you should think about, too. Slouching is not a good idea, leaning your chin on your hand makes you look tired, wild gestures may seem unprofessional, fiddling with a pen is distracting and makes you look nervous (and pointing at people with your pen is especially offensive), smiling occasionally usually makes a candidate more attractive, and so on. You can prepare for these aspects of an interview with a videotape or a coach. During the interview, try to monitor your own behavior and remember your coach's advice.

Candidates often wonder whether they should show the full extent of the enthusiasm or the reservations that they may feel about the position. My observation is that most search committee members, even those who understand that the best candidates may require cultivation of their interest in the position, are put off by people who are not eager to become part of the great institution that the committee represents. I would not encourage candidates who are actually interested in the position to pretend a lack of interest; this is more likely to hurt your candidacy than to help it. On the other hand, if you have serious reservations about the position, I suggest that you express them, but not in a way that dominates the conversation. It is especially unwise to say, "I'm not sure that

I'm interested in the position, but the consultant insisted that I come to interview." This makes the consultant look foolish, but it makes you look bad, too.

CONFIDENTIALITY

Confidentiality is a very important issue for many candidates. They do not want colleagues, especially those on their current campus, to know that they may be interested in moving. At the stage of transmitting a CV and other documents, candidates can claim that they were complying with a request in which they had no real interest. But when you actually get in your car or get on a plane and make a trip to meet with a search committee, it is harder to claim innocence. At this stage, you have to consider whether you are willing to take the risk that your confidentiality will be breached. If you are interviewing at a public institution, you may have few protections against this risk. Media may take an interest in finding out who is being interviewed, or there may be sunshine laws that make all candidate names public. Apart from these hazards, there is simply the likelihood that a committee member, once having met you, is more likely to mention your name thoughtlessly to someone else. If you believe that this is a serious risk, you should be thinking about which of your colleagues needs to hear directly from you that you are talking with a search committee, rather than hearing it from someone else.

There is an exception to the general rule that candidates who go to an interview have lost the ability to deny their own interest in the position. Some committees may be willing to talk with individuals who have not committed to becoming candidates, treating them as "informational" or "exploratory" interviews. In this case, the preliminary interview takes a distinctive tone, in which the committee's effort to recruit the candidate is dominant. While there may be a series of questions, they may be less formal, and the discussion may be more conversational. The candidate may be treated more like a consultant, asked to offer observations about the institution rather than to report on their own prior experience, or the approach to that prior experience may be more in the nature of getting acquainted, and less like a formal review of qualifications. The visitor will be encouraged to ask questions so that the committee can address the concerns that may stand in the way of a candidacy. This is an unusual approach, reserved for candidates who are of very great interest to the committee and who, without this special approach, would simply not be willing to enter into the process at all. Sometimes these individuals are engaged by the conversation and later become active candidates, and sometimes their reservations are confirmed and they decide to go no further in the process.

CHAPTER 4

Second-Round Interviews

Typically only three to five people are invited for the second-round interview. Congratulations on getting to this stage! The first question you have to answer is, do you want to participate? If you have grown increasingly interested in the position, the other significant people in your life are generally prepared to make the adjustments that your move might entail for them, the material elements of the position seem satisfactory (especially compensation) —then you should move ahead. But if you have come to feel that nothing the institution could do would attract you to the position, you should consider withdrawing. If you learn something about the institution or the position at the last minute that is a deal-breaker, that is a perfectly acceptable reason to withdraw at a later stage. But it is very trying for a search committee to move through an elaborate search process with a favorite candidate who, at the very last minute, declines to accept the position when the reason for declining was present from the start. My favorite example of this last-minute realization is the candidate who says, "I have a child who is a junior in high school and I just can't move him at the start of his senior year." Or the candidate who says, "My partner is unwilling to move to a small town in the snowbelt that is three hours from an airport." Such a last-minute change of heart, particularly when, as in these examples, the deciding factor was known from the start, can also hurt your prospects in the future because the search consultant will record this behavior not only in his or her memory but in the consulting firm's database, and committee members, in spite of confidentiality rules, are likely to remember and complain about your behavior as well.

If you decide to accept the invitation to a second-round interview, what can you expect? For vice presidential searches, second-round interviews are typically fairly public events, held on campus, with one or two days of meetings with a wide range of participants, and with the candidates' CVs posted on the institution's Web site. For presidential searches, the interview may be handled more confidentially. I will talk about the public, on-campus interview first, and then about the confidential second-round interview.

PUBLIC SECOND-ROUND INTERVIEWS

On-campus interviews generally follow a similar format from one search to the next, varying only in details. Although presidential candidates may have this public kind of interview, especially in public institutions, I will discuss these interviews in the context of vice presidential searches, where they are more common. Often candidates are asked whether they have particular requests, so you can sometimes influence the shape of the visit. The candidate typically comes to campus, stays at a nearby hotel, and spends one or two full days meeting with key members of the campus community:

- The president;
- All the vice presidents (sometimes individually and sometimes as a group);
- The outgoing vice president, and the interim vice president if he or she is not a candidate for the position;
- The staff of the office in which the position is located;
- The major campus constituencies—the faculty, the staff, the students, the governance bodies (senate, union, staff association, etc.);
- Trustees, and especially those with a particular interest in the portfolio of the position—e.g., candidates for chief student affairs officer are likely to meet with the chair of the board's student affairs committee;
- Other groups or individuals depending on the position and the institution, such as the affirmative action task force, the athletic director, or the director of institutional research;
- The academic department in which an appointment is being considered, if that is a likely element of your appointment.

The most important meetings usually have to do with revenue flow, and if these are not on your schedule, you should request them. Be sure that you meet with the chief financial officer, the chief development officer, and the chief enrollment officer.

The schedule is almost always very demanding. Many members of the campus community want a chance to meet with candidates, and committees usually have a hard time saying no or asking that several groups participate in joint meetings rather than each having its own time with you. Testing your capacity to maintain grace under pressure and alertness in spite of fatigue is part of the drill, as is observing your ability to remember names, respond to complicated or faintly hostile questions, navigate political minefields, make eye contact with your audience, respond equitably to questions from men and women and from groundskeepers and graduate deans. This is a marathon run on a stage.

PREPARING FOR SECOND-ROUND INTERVIEWS

Preparation for the second-round interview is essential, and even more so at this stage because the range of topics is going to be so much broader in a visit that lasts two days rather than two hours. If you are invited to a campus interview, the committee has real interest in you, and you should show your real interest in them by preparing with care. Study all available materials (e.g., Web site, materials sent to you, news reports, and ratings and rankings by outside groups such as U.S. News and World Report and the National Research Council (NRC) rankings of graduate programs). Talk to colleagues who work or previously worked at this institution to learn something about its culture and recent history. If you learn something that links this institution to others where you have worked, you can comment on this, showing how suited you are to the position (for example, "The religious orders that founded our two institutions have a history of significant dialogue and many shared values," or "The concerns raised in your recent accreditation report or campaign feasibility study are very similar to the concerns raised two years ago at my current institution; we were able to deal with the issues so effectively that we now have notable strength in that area").

Talking about Your Vision

One of the things you are likely to be asked is your vision for the area of the institution for which you would be responsible. This is an important question, but it is also a potential trap. Before defining a vision, you probably need to know much more about the institution than you will know before your interview, no matter how well you have prepared. You will not have had the opportunity to listen to the many voices of members of the campus community. You will probably not know enough about recent institutional history and the debates that have occurred around various visions for the future. You may not have sufficient insider information to know what resources are available to fulfill an ambitious vision. How can you possibly answer a question about your vision?

But if you are asked about your vision, you must say something. If you have formulated a vision, and testing campus support for your vision is essential to your accepting the position, then you should lay it out. I have seen a candidate say, "I need to tell you that the vision defined by the previous provost is not one that I share; if I come here, I will want to define the vision differently." In this case, there was mutual agreement between the candidate and the search committee that this candidate would not go forward in the search. But if the outgoing provost had been viewed as having the wrong vision, and the candidate's comment was greeted with enthusiasm, this could have been a very effective approach to the question.

More often, though, candidates do not have enough knowledge at this point of what the vision has been, and have not yet formulated a sense of what they would like it to be. Not answering the question is usually viewed as evasive. You might want to speculate about a vision for this institution, while cautioning that you have a lot more to learn before being certain that this is the right direction to take. Or, you might emphasize what you would want to do before defining a vision (such as how you would get to know the institution better, and how long this might take), and the way that you have shaped the vision in other positions you have held (e.g., "As dean, I defined the vision for the school of business by holding a series of listening sessions with constituents both on and off campus, formulating a white paper, and circulating it for deliberation. This occurred over a six-month period. The revised document was affirmed unanimously by the provost and by the university senate, and a donor whom I had cultivated provided an endowment of $50 million that allowed us to carry out the vision").

Anticipating the Interview Questions

There are other questions and situations that a candidate can anticipate. Because the wide range of participants in an on-campus interview are generally not as organized as the search committee, individual participants in the interview process are likely to ask whatever they wish. You may hear the same questions repeatedly ("Why do you want this job?" "What is your management style?"). You may find yourself telling the same story several times during the interviews, and you should expect audiences to compare notes. If you find your answers shifting in the course of the day, you might want to say, "Since being asked this question earlier, I've thought some more about it and I'd like to approach my answer a little differently this time." Someone will probably interpret this to mean you are indecisive or can't think on your feet, but others will infer that you are reflective and flexible. What you want to avoid is having your interviewers conclude that you manipulatively or opportunistically give different answers to different audiences.

You are also likely to hear questions that reflect the hot controversy of the day, but provide you with less than complete information on which to base your answer, such as "How would you make a tenure decision about someone who is an outstanding and award-winning teacher, but who has only published one article since joining our faculty?" You don't want to venture an answer because you don't know enough of the facts, and of course any answer you give will please half the audience and enrage the rest. But you do not want to evade the question. You might answer in terms of your past experience ("I don't know enough of the facts to say how I would handle that situation, but let me tell you how I handled a similar situation in a previous position"). But be careful with your examples, because if they are too specific ("We had a situation like that in the history department"), some may see you as unable to keep a confidence. You might consider generalizing the question to a level at which it can be addressed adequately ("I think your question is really asking about my views on the balance of teaching, research, and service in making a faculty personnel decision") and then talking about your views on this difficult issue.

SPOUSES AND PARTNERS

Sometimes family members (normally the spouse or partner) are invited to the on-campus interview, and sometimes that step is left until after an offer has been extended. In some cases, this person is never invited. I think it is valuable to invite the spouse or partner to campus sooner in the process rather than later, since often this person is a critical part of deciding whether to accept an offer. But each institution has its own set of expectations on this matter, as well as a variable capacity to absorb additional costs. If your spouse or partner is invited, and there are events planned that include this person (e.g., a dinner meeting to which the president, committee chair, and board chair will be bringing their spouses), you should make every effort to have your spouse or partner attend; if not, questions will be raised about whether you are really interested in the position.

Some spouses enhance your candidacy, and some detract from it. I have seen several interviews at which the spouse was at least as compelling as the candidate and was a substantial asset to the candidacy. But I have also seen interviews in which the spouse was a negative. It is devastating to think that the person you love could unintentionally harm your candidacy. One example is the husband who appeared much smarter and more energetic than his candidate wife, making her look dull and indecisive by contrast and contributing to the committee rejecting her as a candidate. Another example is a wife who was several years older than the candidate husband and already retired, and who appeared to be elderly and feeble. The candidate was relatively old as well but had a youthful demeanor—until the wife became a reminder of how old he actually was. What can you do in a situation like this? The elderly wife might have asked for a schedule that would not leave her weary when the dinner party began, or might have made sure to talk to key people about her lively intellectual interests in order to counterbalance her appearance. The dynamic husband should have kept in mind that his wife should be the center of attention at this event.

Your wardrobe should be attractive, comfortable, and appropriate to the position for which you are a candidate; aspiring presidents need to look presidential, and their spouses need to look like aspiring presidential spouses. When in doubt, err on the conservative side and dress more formally rather than less formally. If you have some sense of how people dress in this community, you should dress the way they do so that your clothing shows you to be a natural member of the community, rather than an outsider.

Many professional associations that serve presidents and vice presidents have established programs to serve spouses and partners, and sessions at annual conferences are an opportunity to meet others in similar situations. Some of these groups discuss the complex issues surrounding professional positions for spouses and partners, as well as providing collegial support. Contacting leaders in these groups may provide a useful resource for candidates.

CONFIDENTIAL SECOND-ROUND INTERVIEWS

Some presidential searches are handled exactly as just described, with full on-campus public interviews. But in other searches, there is no request for candidates to spend a very public day or two on campus meeting with all constituencies. Instead, knowing that some candidates are likely to be sitting presidents at other institutions, these searches use a process that protects the confidentiality of the candidate until a final selection has been made, at which point the new president is introduced to the campus. This approach has both advantages and hazards. Faculty and other constituencies are likely to feel that their opportunity for consultation in the selection process has been limited, with their representatives on the search committee carrying full responsibility for providing their input. Some may argue that the new president has less credibility because no other candidates were presented by way of contrast or competition. From the candidate's perspective, it may be valuable to have one's confidentiality protected, but there is no opportunity to take the measure of the wider campus to get a sense of the culture, behavior, and concerns of those with whom you will be working, and upon whom you will depend for success. The president who is selected by this process may take office under the cloud of an exclusive rather than inclusive governance process.

The Format of a Confidential Second-Round Interview

When confidential second-round interviews are the approach, there is generally a return visit to a confidential location for several hours of interviews with a broader group, but a group still committed to confidentiality. For example, instead of the small number of board members who are on the committee, the full board may be invited to the interview. The full senior staff may be asked to participate in the interviews. The executive committee of the faculty senate may be invited in order to expand the faculty representation in the process. A leadership group of staff or students may be included, and so on. All these individuals are reminded that candidate confidentiality should be maintained both during the search and forever after, just as committee members were advised of this. The increased number of participants makes this promise somewhat harder to keep, but it should be the expectation even so.

In this format, each major constituency group typically spends an hour with each candidate (although some committees prefer to mix the constituency groups together). To bring the search to a rapid conclusion after this step, the three or four finalists may all be interviewed on the same day, with the candidates rotating among the interview groups. At the end of the day of interviews, each group provides its feedback to the committee, which convenes to make a recommendation to the board of trustees. Ideally, the board makes its decision that same day or the next day. Candidates should already have talked with the search consultant, search committee chair, or board chair about the terms of an offer and should have expressed their willingness to accept the position if it is offered—barring their learning something during these interviews that would raise concerns. Ideally, the appointment is confirmed and announced immediately, or certainly very soon after the day of interviews concludes.

The Decision to Hold Open or Closed Interviews

Candidates do not typically have much choice about whether the second-round interview is open or closed. Occasionally, though, a sitting president may tell a search committee that he or she is unwilling to go to the second interview unless confidentiality is assured, and that the full campus visit is thus not acceptable. Often the candidate frames this as, "I will only come to campus if I am the single candidate under consideration, or after an offer has been extended." Sitting presidents with little to gain and a lot to lose from participating in a search process are most likely to raise this issue. The committee must then decide whether to respect this request or to lose the candidate.

Most candidates accept the process as the search committee has defined it—either open or closed. Nonetheless, one might ask which format is preferable from a candidate's perspective. On balance, I think that the open interview holds greater advantage for a candidate. It virtually guarantees loss of confidentiality, but it provides a more naturalistic setting, allowing the candidate to move among different groups over a day or more, with informal conversations between meetings and over meals. The open public interview process is thus more likely to give the candidate the opportunity to show his or her normal style and approach. While any interview is an unnatural setting, the on-campus open interview more closely approximates real life and thus gives the candidate and the institution a better opportunity to test the fit. This interview may be a very stressful experience, and certainly is unnatural in some ways, but in the end it is likely to give you a better chance to show what you know and can do than a more formal interview with a small group.

CHAPTER 5

Building Relationships with Committees and Consultants

The relationship between the candidate and the committee and consultant over the course of the search process can vary tremendously, depending on the personalities and approaches of each of the participants. But some generalizations can be offered. I will begin by discussing the candidate's relationship with the consultant and with the committee chair, and then consider the candidate's relationship with the committee when there is no consultant.

WHAT CANDIDATES CAN EXPECT
DURING THE SEARCH PROCESS

Ideally, candidates can expect to be treated with respect and with recognition for the demands on their time and their need for confidentiality; to be kept current about the progress of the search; to be given all the information they need about the institution and the position; and to be given honest feedback about their candidacy. But even with the best intentions, these things do not always happen.

Search committees often bring with them a "selecting" frame of reference when they should bring a "recruiting" frame of reference. That is, they assume that the best candidates will be eager to have the job, and that the task of the committee members is to pick the best candidate and turn away the others. The reality is that the best candidates often need to be actively recruited and cultivated. This difference in frame of reference can be the source of problems in the search. For example, committee members may grill you when they should also be cultivating your interest. They may fail to give you an opportunity to ask your own questions. They may stick rigidly to their script in ways that make the interview more stilted than it has to be. None of these is a good practice, but any can occur because the search committee defines its role as selecting rather than recruiting.

Candidates may be in a state of considerable anxiety about the progress of a search, and are usually hungry for information about the search process and timetable. While some institutions (typically the public institutions) post the search schedule on a Web site, others are more reticent about their process. Candidates should try to understand that the process may be fluid; recruiting may continue until the committee is satisfied with the candidate pool, and thus it may not be possible to say at the start of a search exactly when it will conclude. Delays in the most carefully planned search schedule may be unavoidable; illness or blizzards or strikes or innumerable other unanticipated events may lead to delays. Thanksgiving through Martin Luther King Day includes a very busy time on any campus, and then many people are absent for vacations, so some searches become stalled during this period.

There are also times when "unanticipated delays" is the excuse given to a candidate who is actually a second or even third choice. While the board chair or the committee chair negotiates with the preferred candidate, the other candidates may be told not that they are second or third choice, but that the search process has slowed down. The committee's fear, of course, is that if candidates knew they were not the first choice, they might withdraw from the search or accept another offer. And there are many "second-choice" candidates who are ultimately appointed and perform with great success, so it is important to retain these people as candidates. These candidates are probably better off never knowing that someone else declined the offer before it was extended to them.

Substantive information about the institution and the position is perhaps the most important element that a candidate normally expects from a search committee. A survey by the American Council on Education reported that "one in five presidents indicated that he or she had not received a full and accurate disclosure of the institution's financial condition."[1] Some newly appointed presidents view this as a matter of deception, caused by the committee's fear that telling the candidates all the painful details would lead them to decline the offer. But it may also be a matter of ignorance. The chief financial officer may or may not know about a financial problem, and may or may not have revealed a financial problem to the search chair or board chair. It is remarkably common that newly appointed presidents, with fresh eyes or a new set of analytical tools, uncover financial problems that no one was previously aware of, including everything from financial fraud to structural deficits. Candidates who are among the two or three finalists should feel free to press for full financial disclosure, as well as for full information about all other issues that are germane to the leadership role they are considering. For additional advice about important information to gather before making a decision, a valuable source is *The Well-Informed Candidate: A Brief Guide for Candidates for College and University Presidencies.*[2]

FEEDBACK ABOUT INTERVIEW PERFORMANCE

Candidates who do not ultimately receive an offer sometimes want feedback about the reasons they were not selected. Some candidates would rather put the process behind them, but others seek information that can help them to be better candidates in future searches. The ability of the consultant or the committee to provide this feedback is highly variable. Some individuals are more comfortable than others with this kind of conversation. Candidates can make the conversation easier by signaling that they have no interest in taking any kind of legal action if the reasons do not satisfy them. If candidates make it clear that their motive is only to be able to do better the next time, getting some useful feedback is more likely.

Feedback can often be very helpful. If, for example, your candidacy was harmed by a poor second-round interview in which your public presentation offended members of the audience or put them to sleep, or in which you were observed to behave inappropriately after too many glasses of wine at dinner, or in which your responses were widely perceived as evasive, you should hear this and think about how you can do better next time. You will only hear this if you ask and if you listen without defensiveness to what you are told.

Whether or not you receive feedback, be cautious about inferring or guessing about the dynamics and politics of the decision-making process. Candidates often look back on searches and say "I was the first choice of the faculty, but the administration opposed me and insisted on the selection of someone else." You may be right, but the chances are that you are wrong. It is rarely as simple as this. Your information sources usually do not have enough information to analyze the politics fully, and often lack the courage to tell you frankly how your performance may have been flawed. Committee members are typically expected to maintain confidentiality about the deliberations both during and after the search, so those with the best understanding may be unwilling to reveal anything at all. Insider political analysis is typically not a fruitful area to pursue.

In seeking feedback, candidates should be prepared for answers they do not like. After making a presentation to a search committee, I was once told that the other candidate was selected over me because "he was so youthful and tan." The age discrimination admitted by this search chair was astonishing, but it offers a valuable lesson for all candidates. The truth may be that you were not selected because you seemed too old or because you were female or because you were gay or because of your race or ethnicity, but you will probably never know for sure. Seeking legal recourse for a claim of illegal discrimination may be an appropriate approach in some situations, but it is a very risky strategy in terms of the advancement of your career. Although I am not aware of enough cases of legal action surrounding executive searches in higher education to formulate a generalization, I can say that search committee reactions are highly unfavorable when they review candidates known to have brought litigation against other institutions.

THE CANDIDATE'S RELATIONSHIP
WITH THE SEARCH CONSULTANT
Consultants Work for the Institution, Not the Candidate

The most important thing for candidates to remember about search consultants is that the consultant does not work for you. Search consultants work for the institution and their loyalty is not to the candidate but to the institution that hired them. The further you move through the process, the more extensive your relationship with the consultant will probably be, but you should not mistake this for loyalty. The consultant must serve the institution and assist it in recruiting the person identified by the appropriate individual or group as the best candidate for the position. No matter how much the consultant supports (or seems to support) your candidacy, in the end it is not the consultant's choice. You want to develop a relationship of mutual understanding and respect with the consultant, but always remember these fundamentals. Consider carefully how much you wish to disclose, and when you want to disclose it. If you confide in the consultant, you can certainly ask him or her to maintain a confidence, but remember where the consultant's loyalty lies. I cannot speak for other consultants, but when I am asked to maintain a confidence, I let candidates know whether I can do so. Often I will respect the confidence but also try to formulate a statement that the candidate is willing to have conveyed to the search chair or committee, thus respecting the candidate's wishes as well as my responsibility to my client.

Consultants Need Strong Candidates

Having said this, I must also say that the consultant can only be successful if the candidates are strong, and are perceived by the search committee to be strong. Thus, a search consultant has an interest in your strength as a candidate. Some will give you advice on your written materials. For example, if I see a potentially attractive candidate who has written what I believe to be a weak letter, I may encourage him or her to revise it. Or, if I see a candidate about to be interviewed who has some gaps in his or her background, I may coach that candidate to improve preparation. This can take the form of areas for study—e.g., "Since you have never worked in a church-related institution before, you need to talk to colleagues in that kind of institution who can help you to grasp the issues you would face if you become chief advancement officer." If I see a candidate whose skills are excellent but whose self-presentation may be troublesome in an initial interview, I may suggest a different approach, such as, "This is a very urbane and sophisticated institution, and your string tie/pink suit/beard/cowboy boots may make you look like an outsider." If you are fortunate enough to be working with a consultant who is willing and able to give you this kind of coaching, pay attention.

If you are moving forward in the search but no advice has been offered, you can ask for advice. It may not be given, but it does not hurt to ask. You might ask about your written materials, about your reference list, about how best to prepare for the preliminary interview and the second-round interview, about your appearance and demeanor, about feedback from each stage in the process, about gaps or flaws in your background that you will need to address and strengths that you might emphasize, and so on. I am not suggesting asking about all these things, but selective questions are fine. If the consultant appears eager to assist you, you can try some other questions, but be cautious about making excessive demands.

One hazard of excessive requests for guidance is that you become a high-maintenance candidate. The stronger you are as a candidate, the more you can expect from the consultant and the more demands you can make. If you are a weak candidate—e.g., a presidential candidate who has only been an associate dean, or a candidate for chief advancement officer who has only worked on the annual fund and has never managed staff—the consultant will probably see that no matter how much coaching you get, you will not move very far in this search. Investing time in supporting you may have long-term value in strengthening your presidential candidacy for five or 10 years from now, but it does not serve the institution who hired the consultant. But if you are a potentially strong candidate—e.g., a sitting president at a peer institution who is considering a second presidency, or a provost candidate who has been a successful dean at an institution of greater stature than the one that is searching—the consultant is serving the institution doing the search by spending time with you, building a relationship with you on behalf of the institution, and helping you to address areas of concern that could keep the search committee from seeing your considerable strength.

One of the ironies of the search process is that the weakest candidates often make the most demands—phoning to be sure that their materials arrived, asking the consultant to review a cover letter and suggest revisions, and sending messages with all contact information that might be needed while the candidate is away at a conference. Before you do these things—and especially before you do more than one of them—be sure that you are viewed as a serious contender in this search.

EVALUATING AND IMPROVING
YOUR STRENGTH AS A CANDIDATE
Signals to the Strong Candidates

How do you know if you are a serious contender? Consultants may tell you this directly, or may send subtle signals. They (or their assistants) may phone to thank you for your interest or to see if you have questions, or they may offer to send you additional materials about the institution. They may ask to talk with you at length by phone to get to know you better, or to have a video interview with you, or to meet you in person. They may invite you to meet with the search committee or other representatives of the institution. If you get one or more of these signals, the consultant is probably considering whether you are a serious contender.

Identifying Flaws in Your Candidacy

If you fail to get any positive signals in several searches, you should consider what is happening. You may be looking too soon in your career, without enough experience to prepare you for the positions you want. If you are young enough, time is on your side; get more experience and try again in a few years. If you do not want to wait, or if you are older and cannot afford to wait to make a move, you should consider whether your institutional or position aspirations are too high. You may be a weak candidate for chief financial officer at an institution with a $500 million budget, but you might be more attractive at an institution with a $100 million budget. Or you may be a weak candidate for a presidency, but a strong candidate for a provost position. You will of course need to decide whether making this adjustment in your expectations is worth it; you might fulfill one aspect of your career goal (becoming a vice president) but not another (being at an institution with a budget of $500 million).

If you repeatedly move forward to a certain point in the search process but not further, analyze where the trail runs cold and consider the potential areas needing improvement. For example, if your written materials are sufficiently well received that you are invited to have a conversation with the consultant, but you never get a committee interview, reflect on that conversation. Perhaps you were asked questions to which you really had no good answer—for instance, "What experience have you had working with legislators? With donors? With collective bargaining"? In this situation, you may need to find ways to build the requisite experience, or to adjust your search strategy so that you focus on institutions where this will not be a concern. You might also think about what answers you offered that the consultant may have found unsatisfactory—e.g., "Tell me about a situation in which you have provided a vision for your area of responsibility"; or, "Can you describe the way you handle difficult decisions?" The problem is less often that you gave a "wrong" answer, and more often that you were unable to provide a convincing answer. For example, if you answer the question about vision by describing your approach to an operational problem, you are implying that you either do not understand the concept of vision or have never been asked to shape a vision. In a presidential search, that is a serious omission. If you describe the handling of a difficult decision in a way that suggests you ultimately delegated the answer to a committee, you are implying that you cannot take responsibility yourself and must have a process that protects you from the controversy. In these kinds of situations, consider whether you have accurately described your experience. Perhaps you have made difficult decisions but were not able to quickly come up with a good example or an effective way of describing it. Consider too whether you accurately described your experience and your approach, but in fact that approach is not going to be a good fit for the particular institution whose presidency or vice presidency you are considering; there are likely many other institutions where you would be a better fit.

In addition to substance, there are matters of style that can cause your candidacy to be derailed at the interview stage, either with the consultant or with the committee. Review the chapter about interviews to get some ideas about what may be going wrong and how you can do better. Interview style is perhaps the most potentially damaging element in the search process, when very good candidates may turn in a weak performance even though they would really be an excellent fit for the position.

Problems with References

If your candidacy has more than once ended after references are checked, one or more of your references may be undermining your candidacy. It could be someone on your reference list, or it could be someone who was contacted after you gave permission to call people not listed as references. In either case, this is a serious problem, exacerbated by the fact that you may not be certain who is harming you. If a listed reference is not supporting you enthusiastically, you should of course avoid listing him or her as a reference. Committees are always somewhat uneasy when they receive weak references, but this is especially true if the individual is listed as a reference. It may be difficult to remove this person from your list if the reference is your supervisor or someone else whose observations will be virtually required before you are selected. But even delaying the committee's conversation with this person can help your case. If committee members have heard a lot of good things about you before hearing these negative comments, they may be better able to take them in stride, whereas negatives at an earlier stage can be more damaging.

You can always hope that there is just one person who is speaking against you and that the next search committee will not happen to call that person. But you should think carefully about whether the problem may be deeper than that and may call for a solution other than simply hoping for better luck next time. Think about the nature of your relationship with this reference and what is likely to be his or her concern. If it is a broad personality trait (e.g., lack of charisma, openness, or determination), it is likely that others will have similar observations about you. Your best approach may be to look for opportunities in which this description will not be a concern, or in which your good qualities will be given greater weight. If it is a character trait (e.g., integrity), it will be very hard to combat; even one claim of lack of integrity can be fatal to your candidacy. But many descriptions of personality and character can be tied to a particular situation, and you may be able to find a way of talking about this situation that provides the committee with a different perspective. For example, someone may be telling the committee that you were not honest about the handling of a personnel decision. Your view may be that the institution's policies prohibited you from providing the full disclosure that you would have liked to provide. Perhaps you can find someone who can provide a reference who was a participant in this situation and is able to confirm your perspective. Perhaps you can tell the story yourself before the committee hears it in a reference report, providing them with some context in which to evaluate the information. Simply telling a story like this directly to the search committee is often seen as a sign of integrity and may inoculate you from the impact of the negative reference.

For some people, candidacy moves to the final stage in which references have been checked and there has been a second-round interview. The decision then rests with the final decision maker (the president or the board), but you are not selected in several searches. If your candidacy is repeatedly derailed at this stage, it may simply be a matter of continuing to seek positions until the stars align and you are selected. But meanwhile, you should find out who was selected and make a clear-eyed appraisal of your qualifications compared to his or hers. The person appointed to a presidency may have had more fund-raising experience, for example; the person appointed chief advancement officer may have had more experience with larger major gift solicitations, or with staffing a very demanding president; the person appointed chief student affairs officer may have been at an institution with an excellent reputation for diversity and a sense of campus community. While you wait for the next search opportunity, strive to build your skills in the areas that made the selected candidate stronger than you.

THE CANDIDATE'S RELATIONSHIP WITH THE SEARCH COMMITTEE

When the search committee is working without a consultant, there is often a strong relationship between the candidate and the committee, especially the chair. When there is a consultant, the relationship between the candidate and the search committee is typically limited, especially in the early stages of the search. But even when they are using a consultant, some search chairs make a special effort to connect with their candidates and provide insider answers to their questions, but most chairs are happy and relieved to have a consultant to whom they can assign this responsibility.

Search chairs who build a direct relationship with candidates will typically get very good results. They get to know the candidates and are able to make an appraisal of them from an earlier point in the process. They can cultivate the strongest candidates in a way that the consultant could not (e.g., the search chair may invite the candidate to join him at a major event, such as the president's box at a major institutional sporting event). They can provide information and insights that may go beyond the consultant's knowledge (e.g., political details of recent institutional controversies, or budget projections not otherwise made public). Candidates typically respond extremely well to the attention received from the actual decision maker, and even when the insider information provided may raise concerns for the candidate, the privilege of being given the information is valued. The interaction between the candidate and the committee chair or board chair is an opportunity to test and build a relationship that may be critical to a successful tenure in the position, especially when, for example, the presidential candidate gets to know the trustee who is chairing the search committee and who will soon become the board chair.

The candidate may also have the opportunity to talk individually with members of the search committee. A candidate for chief financial officer may ask for or be offered the chance to talk with the trustee chair of the finance committee. The value of this kind of relationship during the search process is similar to the link between candidate and search chair.

In some searches, very strong prospective candidates are offered "hospitality visits" outside the framework of the normal series of interviews. Individuals who are being actively recruited, or applicants viewed as very strong candidates, may be invited to come to campus and get better acquainted with key institutional leaders. The candidate's family may be invited to participate in the visit, creating an excellent recruiting opportunity that includes real estate tours, cultural tours, opportunities to see the local schools, and so on. If the visit is handled badly, or the candidate or family members become aware of more negatives than positives, this strategy can backfire from the institution's perspective, but from the candidate's perspective it is probably far better to have learned about these negatives sooner rather than later. But normally these visits are carefully orchestrated by the institution and serve to make the candidate even more attracted to the position.

NOTES

1. Melanie E. Corrigan, *The American College President* (Washington, DC: American Council on Education, 2002), 45–46.

2. Robert H. Atwell, Madeleine F. Green, and Marlene Ross, *The Well-Informed Candidate: A Brief Guide for Candidates for College and University Presidencies* (Washington, DC: American Council on Education, n.d.).

CHAPTER 6

Considering an Offer

All the complexities and demands of the search process sometimes lead to an offer, and for most candidates this is a cause for instant celebration! But sometimes this moment brings greater consternation than one might expect. If you are the candidate who is asked to accept a presidency or vice presidency, you have a very important decision to make. Many people are affected by your decision, including your family, your current colleagues, the new institution, and the other candidates. There will be pressure on you to decide quickly, and in fact some finalists are asked even before a winner is selected to state that they will accept the position if it is offered. The process that surrounds the offer—how it is made, how generous it is, how it is negotiated—can have long-lasting reverberations, and it should be handled with care.

DECIDING WHETHER TO ACCEPT

You should have decided earlier in the process if you are really interested in this position. Candidates who apply for a position on their own typically have a strong interest, but even a direct applicant may learn things during the search process that cause reservations. This is entirely legitimate. You should not feel obliged to accept a position if the second-round interviews and additional conversations with board members or other institutional leaders have given you significant concerns. Gather all the information you can about the institution before you decide whether to accept—find out about what the faculty, staff, and students are like, what the long-term controversies have been, how governance really works, and whatever else you feel you need to know. You also should not feel obliged to accept if the offer is not adequate. Consider, though, whether the gap between your hopes and the actual offer is large enough to justify giving up an otherwise attractive position, and consider how likely you are to get an offer from another institution that will be closer to your hopes.

Many candidates can count on their instincts to tell them whether the fit of this opportunity is good. They will say that they like the people and the culture, and that they know how to deal with and want to deal with the issues the institution faces. They say that they are eager to live in this location, and that their whole family is prepared to make the move. A candidate fitting this description may decide to simply trust his or her instincts, supplemented by all the research he or she has done about the institution and the position, and accept the offer.

But some people should not trust their instincts. They may be so thrilled to (finally) have an offer that they overlook toxic or intrusive board members, intractable campus relationships that led to the firing of the previous president, or institutional aspirations that wildly exceed the institution's capacity. On the other hand, some candidates may be by instinct reluctant to take a leap; they may need to push themselves to try something new, even though it may entail some risks. Only you will know which description applies to you.

Some candidates will want to make lists of pros and cons, or lists of deal-breaking issues. For example, the location may be very attractive but the compensation package may make it impossible for you and your family to live at the level that you wish. Your family may be staying behind for a year or more and you might request support for travel expenses. On the professional level, you may be seeking a vice presidency but ultimately want a presidency, and you might be attracted to a position that promises valuable mentoring by the president, as well as an understanding that you will begin your next search after four years as vice president.

Expectations for the president and his or her partner can be a key element in the attractiveness of the position. There may be very traditional expectations for the presidential spouse. If you are a dual-career couple, you and your spouse will need to decide whether you are willing to take on a more traditional lifestyle for the period of this presidency and, if not, whether you can reasonably hope that the institution will come to accept your approach. There are some institutions where the situation is reversed. You may define the relationship with your husband or wife as a "copresidency" or at least a very close partnership, but the institution may feel that he or she should stay out of institutional matters. Candidates with same-sex partners will want to consider how open they wish to be about this relationship, and the role that the partner will play in the life of the institution. In all these cases, be sure that you and your family have a general sense of comfort with the expectations of the institution.

In some searches, the consultant, committee chair, or board chair may ask two or more finalists whether they would accept the position if it is offered. This is a difficult position to be in, especially if you may be seeking a salary beyond the expected range, or if you have conditions that may be difficult to meet (such as a tenured position for your spouse or partner). Candidates in this situation may wish to avoid any commitment until they have received an offer, when their hand seems stronger. It is also a difficult situation psychologically; if you do not get the offer, you may want to be able to tell yourself that you really did not want it anyway. Certainly it is fair to say that the things that you learn in the final phases of the selection process may change your mind and make you less inclined to accept an offer (e.g., a dinner with the board chair prior to the final selection may reveal that he drinks excessively, has questionable financial dealings, plans to micromanage your presidency from his office next door, or is simply unpleasant to work with), and the balance of your thinking may shift away from acceptance of the offer.

Dealing with Multiple Offers

It is complicated enough to have one offer and one decision to make, but some candidates find themselves with more than one offer, as well as a counteroffer from their current institution. In an ideal world, all these options are on the table at once, but more often they are sequenced, i.e., you have one offer today, and you are in another search that will select its preferred candidate in three weeks. The offer on the table requires a response in one week. There is no simple way to resolve these dilemmas, but there are some things to think about. How much do you want each position? If the current offer is more attractive than any other you might receive, your decision is simple, but usually the potential offer has significant appeal. Think hard about how much appeal it really has and whether it is worth waiting for, with the risk that you will end up with neither position.

Another approach is to try to get some feedback about the potential offer from the search chair or consultant. Let them know that you have received another offer to which you must respond. They may signal you that their offer is a very strong possibility and urge you to wait, or they may try to speed up their search process because of your time constraints. Listen carefully to the responses; the consultant or chair may also encourage you to accept the offer you already have because their offer is likely to go to someone else and they are trying to protect you from ending up with nothing. Finally, you can try to get the decision period for the offer extended by a couple of weeks—but remember that there is someone just like you waiting to hear from the search committee and wondering why the process is taking so long.

NEGOTIATING FOR INSTITUTIONAL RESOURCES

Assembling the resources necessary to do the job is an essential element of any senior position. Some candidates see the moment when an offer is on the table as the best moment to clarify the need for additional resources and to get assurances of their availability.

Some presidential candidates considering an offer use this opportunity to highlight their expectations for board support. Having been offered the presidency, you may wish to say to the board that the institutional aspirations that you all share can only be achieved if board contributions are significantly increased, setting the pace for an extraordinarily ambitious capital campaign.

You may wish to make it clear to board members that you will only accept the position if they will commit to significantly increasing their gifts.

The President's House

A very important but potentially explosive institutional resource is the president's house. The house is a central element of the president's personal life, and it is also likely to be the setting for very important donor development and community events. But previous presidents may not have kept the house looking its best, or the house may not be suited to these kinds of activities. The candidate considering the offer of a presidency may want to stipulate that purchase of a new house by the institution, or upgrading of the existing house, is a condition of acceptance of the offer. A candidate should do this with the greatest caution and awareness of the risks.

Ideally, the board has addressed all issues associated with the house before the offer is even extended, relieving the president of the political burden of doing so. But if the house is going to incur costs during the term of the new president, either for purchase or for upgrading, the costs should be handled with extreme care. There are many approaches to managing these costs. For example, the board can set out a budget in advance, with a rationale that clearly shows the potential to attract additional institutional resources, and not simply an enhanced lifestyle for the president and his or her family. A committee of the board can oversee unusual or unusually large expense items, such as a home theater, a lap pool, a high-end kitchen, or an elevator. Systematic efforts can be made, once the home is ready, to use it for high-profile donor- or community-related events, in order to demonstrate the institutional value of the enhancement.

A very different situation is the potential president who does not wish to live in the house that has always been the president's residence. This might be because the president is a single person who wants his or her social life to be less visible to students and colleagues. Or it might be because the house is too small for the president's family, or because it is located on a noisy busy street or near the site of many student parties. Whatever the circumstances in each situation, it is essential to give careful attention to all matters associated with the president's house; there are few issues that can spin so quickly out of control in the early months of a presidency, and all these issues should be addressed as part of reviewing and accepting an offer.

Personnel Decisions

Another typical investment of new institutional resources for a new president is the creation of new senior staff positions, sometimes as part of an administrative reorganization. It can be a good idea to raise these issues as part of the negotiation process, but it incurs certain risks as well. On the negative side, a board that is investing a great deal in the transition to a new president (e.g., paying a salary higher than they had paid your predecessor and higher than they had expected to pay, and also likely paying a substantial fee to the search consultant), may become edgy at the thought of creating an expensive new position such as a vice president for planning or chief of staff. On the positive side, creation of the position may be viewed favorably because it symbolizes the new direction that you and the board are setting for the institution (e.g., increasing extramural support by creating a vice president for research, or addressing regional concerns by creating a vice presidency for economic development), or because it frees you to become more fully involved in fund-raising (e.g., creating the position of chief operating officer or executive vice president who can take care of internal management issues while you are off campus meeting with donors). Consider whether the creation of a new position is an essential element of your package, or something that will be part of the planning process over the first year or two as you examine the current use of resources and consider a range of priorities and possible reallocation of resources.

There may also be some members of the senior leadership team or the president's office staff whom you wish to remove. In many cases, you will not know this before accepting the position. But it is still worthwhile to learn whether any of these individuals are going to be protected by trustees or other key constituencies. Talk with the board chair about any limitations on your ability to build your own team.

FAMILY ISSUES

Family members should have been brought into the search process before there is an offer, but sometimes the institution does not support this; some institutions will say that, once the offer is extended, the selected candidate will be invited to bring his or her family to visit the campus. These institutions often regret this approach because it delays the decision of the candidate who has been offered the job. But sometimes the search process was not the problem; it may be that the candidate's family has not fully come to terms with the possibility of getting this offer, or with the potential disruption its acceptance would entail, and their decision-making process is still at an early stage. Even though they may have visited the campus, they may not have really thought about what it would mean to leave a job, friends, family, and the familiar and satisfying lives they have been leading. Children can present particularly difficult issues but they are quite unpredictable; they may say they can not bear the thought of moving, but if forced to move by a family decision they may surprise everyone by thriving. It can be hard for parents to insist on a move in the face of tears and tantrums, but many parents have found that things work out differently from what the child anticipates—sometimes for better, and sometimes for worse. Your aging parents may have encouraged you to consider this attractive career move, but when the time comes for you to discuss moving 1,000 miles away, they may balk. These considerations can be difficult to deal with before the offer is on the table, but the more you can anticipate your response to an offer, the better your decision making will go if that offer is made.

COMPENSATION AND CONTRACTUAL ISSUES

The compensation package is surely a central feature of any job offer. During the search process, many college and university administrators will say that they did not go into this line of work to get rich, and that money is not their deciding factor. But when the offer is formulated, they may discover a greater interest in compensation than they had earlier indicated. No one likes to take a cut in pay, so a current salary that is high may make a new offer look less attractive. There are many institutions that pay high salaries in part because they believe —correctly—that high salaries make their senior administrative team much less likely to be attracted to other offers. Some candidates are less than forthright during the search process about their salary expectations, hoping that when an offer is made they will have the upper hand and be able to request and to get a better salary than the institution had planned to pay. In general it may be true that a higher salary will be offered than the institution had initially anticipated. But I have seen several candidates whose salary demands during compensation negotiations were not met; the institution withdrew the offer and offered the position to someone else. Do not assume that you hold all the cards in compensation discussions. It depends on many things, including whether there is an attractive candidate waiting in the wings who will accept a more modest offer.

The compensation package can vary widely. Some institutions (particularly regional public institutions) may offer a salary defined within a narrow and pre-determined range, and the same benefits provided to all employees. Others may offer a much more complex package that includes deferred compensation, pay for performance (i.e., bonuses), club memberships, renovation and redecoration of the president's house, a car for both business and personal use, a spousal appointment and/or travel support for the presidential spouse or partner under certain conditions, entertainment allowances, paid board memberships, golden handcuffs that provide special compensation if you are still on the job in five years, and more. Appendix D contains a detailed list of items to consider as you review an offer.

Almost all institutions have legal counsel review the contract or salary letter, and candidates should do the same. A lawyer can be sure that all critical issues are considered before an agreement is signed (e.g., spousal compensation; pro-cess for evaluation, renewal, and salary adjustment; and deferred compensation). The candidate's lawyer can clarify key elements of the agreement (e.g., what "termination without cause" means), and can be sure that important issues are addressed that might otherwise be overlooked (e.g., how performance evaluation will be handled). Using a lawyer to negotiate the agreement is less common, but doing so can be helpful in many ways, particularly if the negotiations are potentially difficult. If the candidate and the institution work with a presidential compensation specialist, he or she should be able to provide comparable salary data that puts this offer into a larger context. For some institutions, comparable salary information is available from other sources, such as a network of peer institutions.

CHAPTER 7

If You Are Not Selected

Sometimes the search process does not lead to an offer. Some candidates decide that they have dodged a bullet, concluding that the institution is seriously troubled, resources are not adequate to the needs, donors and alumni are disaffected, the board is dysfunctional—and all in all, you can and will do better in some other search. But in most cases there is personal disappointment and public awkwardness. To deal with personal disappointment, it is useful to prepare yourself for this possibility, and to give yourself some time to get used to the outcome. I have seen candidates (and this applies particularly to internal candidates) who are so confident that the offer will be theirs that they never really consider the possibility that they will not be selected. Make sure that you have thought about the possibility that the offer will go to someone else, and how you will handle it. In particular, consider whether you want to or will be able to return to your previous position, working with someone else who has been appointed to the position you wanted.

Some candidates ask the search consultant or chair to give them the opportunity to withdraw from the search rather than be rejected by the institution. In some cases this will be permitted, but not always. If all the finalists except the person appointed were known to have withdrawn from the search, it would appear that the person appointed was the only surviving candidate, weakening his or her standing and undermining the perceived effectiveness of the search process. You can ask if you may withdraw before the appointment is announced, but you cannot count on being given this opportunity.

Once you get the news, there are some people who will be waiting to hear it, and who should hear it from you before they hear it from someone else. These are likely to be family members, close colleagues, and references. What will you tell them? Some unsuccessful candidates will tell others how much they wanted the job and how disappointed they are. Others will say they had been considering withdrawing from the process anyway, having increasingly perceived a lack of fit with the institution's culture. Some will say that they were honored to have been a candidate at such a fine institution, even though they regret not getting the job. Some will focus on the person who did get the job, saying that he or she has outstanding credentials and experience and clearly won the position on the merits—or that the person appointed is a loser who will bring the institution to the brink of disaster. Some will say that they heard the selection process was politicized and the board chair's cousin was an old friend of the new president's golfing buddy, or that they faculty supported their candidacy but was overruled by the board. Some will say that they are devastated by the news and need some time to think it through. Probably every story has some elements of truth and some elements of fabrication. Think about your story with care; the gracefulness with which you lose will tell others a lot about you.

If the news really has wounded you, give yourself some time to reflect on it. Do not make any other important decisions for a few days and, in particular, do not decide that you will never be a candidate in another such search; over a period of time your feelings may change. If you cannot trust yourself to tell your story to others in the way that reflects your best self, try to avoid telling the story for a few days.

LEARNING FROM THE EXPERIENCE

Once you have regained your balance, try to learn something from this search experience. Many different kinds of things can be learned. Some may be unique to this situation—for instance, your second-round interview may have occurred on your first day back on your feet after being sick for a week, and you did not have the energy to present yourself effectively. But other lessons may be very valuable as you continue to seek a presidency or vice presidency. Often these have to do with the interview, the single most critical moment in the search process in which good candidates can stumble. Review the chapter on interviewing and try to learn to interview more effectively, either through your own reflection or through seeking help from colleagues or professional workshops. Sometimes you discover that a key element of experience was lacking in your background, while the winning candidate brought strength in that area; consider whether you can use the coming months to strengthen the missing elements of your background in preparation for the next search (e.g., get more fund-raising experience, participate more actively in legislative lobbying, take a leadership role in building institutional partnerships, or working with community leaders). Although I do not want to suggest that you chase after something to fill every gap in your background, there are some shortcomings that are serious and likely to remain barriers to your professional advancement unless you address them.

Some candidates may learn that the lack of a doctoral degree was a barrier to their selection. Those with academic backgrounds are unlikely to have this problem because they will usually have a doctoral degree, but candidates with backgrounds in finance, advancement, and student affairs may face this question when they seek a presidency. Some presidential searches stipulate that an earned doctoral degree is required. Having the degree thus allows you to be a candidate in more searches, but will it actually help you to win the position? That is difficult to know. If you decide to seek a doctoral degree, should it be a Ph.D. or an Ed.D.? These are significant personal decisions, calling for a substantial investment of time and money. What you do depends on your interests, your resources, and your career goals and timetable. All other things being equal, having the degree will probably help. But be sure that you have successfully addressed whatever other limitations may be associated with your candidacy; otherwise they may continue to hold you back even after you have earned the doctoral degree.

Getting feedback about the strengths of your candidacy, and about the limitations that others perceived, can be valuable. How can you get this feedback? The search consultant is most likely to be able to tell you where you fell short and how you might improve, and the chair of the search committee can sometimes be helpful as well. You may hear that there were reservations about your energy level, and observers may encourage you to show the dynamism that better reflects your normal demeanor. The consultant or the chair may tell you that the selection turned on experience with capital campaigns, which you lack; getting that experience can make you a stronger candidate. And the consultant may be able to suggest types of searches in which you are more likely to be successful, such as institutions more like the ones at which you have served in the past, or institutions that will value some of your distinctive strengths, such as your strong international background.

Sometimes feedback can be tougher, such as telling you that your comments during meetings seemed to have racist undertones and offended many in the university community, or seemed arrogant or pretentious, or that you seemed obsessed with institutional rankings or used vulgar language. Sometimes feedback can be more about the politics of the situation, such as controversy among the faculty over whether academic depth or community visibility or fund-raising ability is most important in a president. Be especially wary of the kind of feedback that takes the form, "My group thought you were wonderful, but the trustees rejected our recommendation." This kind of statement allows the speaker to be supportive of you and regretful that you did not get the job, blaming the selection on someone else; such a statement may be convenient and comfortable, but not always accurate.

There is an important grain of salt that should be present as you hear all this. While this institution's search participants may have found you long-winded or low in energy, another institution's search committee next week or next month may find you charming and thorough and appropriately reflective. You are who you are, and the issue may be not presenting yourself differently, but finding an institution that will value the person you are. Sometimes it is just a matter of time before you find that institution.

SPECIAL ISSUES FOR INTERNAL CANDIDATES

If you were an internal candidate (and especially if you held the interim position), you have some especially difficult decisions to make. Will you stay at the institution or do you feel you must leave? Will you return to your previous position (e.g., if you served as interim president, you may or may not want to return to your previous role as provost)? Many candidates assume that, if not selected, they will simply have to leave. This may be true, but it is not necessarily true. Whether you should stay or go depends on personal factors; some candidates are so dismayed by the rejection that they cannot stand to see the chosen candidate in the role that they wanted. It also depends on the person appointed to the position; some may encourage you to stay on and thus to contribute to the stability of the organization, while others may encourage you to move on because of discrepant styles or bad chemistry, or because they wish to appoint their own team. In some cases, this preference for your departure is unspoken, or kept quiet for a period, but you should be alert to the possibility that it is lurking beneath the surface so that you are not blindsided when it is revealed; you will want to start looking for other opportunities before you are told to clear out your desk. Sometimes, the person appointed has obvious strengths that exceed those of the internal candidate, and the appointment provides an excellent opportunity for you to stay and to work with and learn from the person who was selected.

CHAPTER 8

Transition to the New Appointment

n a certain sense, the new presidency or vice presidency begins when the candidate first encounters the search committee. But from a public perspective, the appointment and transition are defining moments for the new leader's time in office. These steps should be managed with care.

ANNOUNCING THE APPOINTMENT

Announcement of the appointment calls for collaboration between the candidate's current institution and the hiring institution. As the person appointed, you have some key decisions to make. Think first about your current institution, considering who needs to hear the news from you directly before a press release is distributed by your new institution. You will need to make a lot of calls, which may take a few days; the more quickly this is done, the better, since word is likely to leak out. To speed the process, consider which calls can be handled instead as e-mail messages.

While you are taking care of these personal responsibilities, the people in charge of media relations at both institutions can be working on a press release. You may want to set the tone for the message and then let the PR people do their work. Make sure that everything the press release says about you is true and fully accurate. Sometimes a reader unfamiliar with your CV can select a relatively minor accomplishment for major emphasis, or describe a shared accomplishment as wholly your own. Be meticulous about accuracy in all these elements.

WORKING WITH YOUR PREDECESSOR

Your relationship with your predecessor will be reflected in the press release as well as in many other things that you will say and do. No matter how widely scorned this person may have been, there is little value in your publicly disparaging him or her. The press release should reflect on the strong foundation that was built by this person, his or her hard work on behalf of the institution and loyalty to its cause, and so on. This is especially important if your predecessor was an internal person who held an interim appointment in the position to which you have just been appointed. You may in fact plan to undo just about everything that your predecessor did, but you do not need to say that in the press release.

Your personal relationship with your predecessor is more complex. Most new presidents recognize that they have something to learn from their predecessors, but few are eager for them to take up long-term residence in an office down the hall. In the worst case, the board has decided, without consulting you, to appoint the outgoing president to a formal role that continues for more than a few months. Boards that see the strong and extensive bonds that the outgoing president has formed with donors or corporate partners are reluctant to give up this asset. Or board members may have personal bonds of loyalty to the outgoing president and want to take care of him or her in some substantial way. There may be long-term complex issues of legislative relations or property acquisition or litigation, and the board may feel that the outgoing president needs to stay around long enough to deal with those issues. The outgoing president may be perceived as such a wonderful person that he or she could never be seen as a threat to a new president—but the new president may not see it that way! If there is a consultant working on the search, he or she should have explained to the board already the concerns that any new president is likely to have about the continuing presence of the predecessor. As the new president, you will certainly want to spend some time with your predecessor to hear his or her insights and to discuss unfinished items that will need your attention. But if you want to clear the decks of the previous administration, you should make the board chair aware of this and ask for support. Some board members may have loyalty not only to your predecessor but to other members of the senior team. Talk directly with the board chair, making clear your need to assemble the leadership team and to set the agenda and style of your new administration.

In most cases, the board has not appointed the outgoing president to a formal role, but he or she may still be a presence on the campus. The successor must decide whether this person represents a significant threat, someone able to rally opposition the first time you make a difficult decision or a misstep, or whether on the other hand this person may be a great resource to you, helping to provide insights and introductions and support when challenges appear.

WORKING WITH INTERNAL CANDIDATES

If there were internal candidates in the search, you will also need to decide how to work with them. As with your predecessor, they can be a resource or a threat. Consider the nature of the search process and the level of controversy or acrimony that may have surrounded it; if an internal candidate was part of that controversy, perhaps because he or she was supported by a significant campus constituency, you might want to placate that constituency by treating your competitor with particular respect, or you may want to make clear your own authority by encouraging that person to leave the institution. Consider the skills of your competitor and his or her place in the institution's history. This person can be an excellent fit with you and provide stability for your administration, or he or she may be incompetent and need to be replaced promptly. In all these situations, it is impossible to decide without knowing the details of the situation; you should consider all the alternative interpretations and options.

OTHER IMPORTANT RELATIONSHIPS

There are many other people with whom you need to build relationships. For a new president, there is no group more important than your board (or, for a new campus head within a system, the head of the system). Get to know these people individually as well and as soon as you can. The search committee chair often becomes the board chair, allowing you to build on the relationship developed during the search. Many new presidents find it valuable to attend workshops designed for the president and the board chair as a way of building that relationship. Consider how you want to work with the executive committee and the full board; the start of your presidency is an opportunity to reflect on frequency of meetings and their agendas, committee structure, the composition of the board and the selection process, term limits, and so on. Although many on-campus issues may be clamoring for your attention, do not fail to focus attention on the board. There are many books and conferences on this topic, and more experienced presidents who can provide guidance and support as you navigate these waters.

New presidents sometimes are surprised by the extent of attention paid to their every move and every word. You may want to be cautious or bold. Whatever you do, do it with the awareness that nothing you do will be without meaning; consider what meaning you want to convey so that you do not accidentally convey the opposite of what you had intended. Whom you talk to, whose advice you seek, how you shape your communication (making phone calls and appointments yourself or having an administrative assistant place your calls and schedule your time; whether you address others by first name or by title, and how you prefer to be addressed by others)—all these will be duly noted and extensively interpreted, so give them some thought in advance.

What kind of continuing relationship should a new president or vice president have with a search committee? If this was a strong, well-respected and representative committee, you may want to continue to draw upon the value of the group. A celebratory event may have been held soon after your selection but before you arrived on campus. You can always schedule another. But you might also want to consider using the search committee as an informal advisory group. They will know better than most of your new colleagues what your position entails and the agenda that has been set for you. They will know your style and your strengths and weaknesses, having heard a lot about you from your references. If you do well, committee members will brag years later that they selected you. If you do badly, they will not be quite so proud, wondering how they could have been so blind.

Everyone at the institution is likely to have some level of interest in and even anxiety about the appointment of a new president, and most will have some interest in a vice presidential appointment as well. But there is a group that will have intense interest, and that is the staff that works most closely with the new appointee—administrative office staff who must work comfortably with their new boss, individuals in "special assistant" roles whose value to your predecessor was that they could anticipate his or her views on all key issues and thus could act on their behalf, schedulers and office managers who have become used to running the office in a certain way. Only you can decide who stays and who goes, but the sooner you are clear with your inherited staff as to how and when you will make these decisions, the more you can reduce the level of anxiety in your office and get everyone back to working effectively in the service of the institution.

The other officers who report directly to you—the vice presidents who report to the president, and the directors and deans who report to the vice presidents—generally take one of two approaches. One approach is to maintain a commitment to the institution, to form a good working relationship with you, and to seek to stay on in their positions. Another approach is to anticipate that they may not want to stay or may not be welcome to stay, and to seek opportunities elsewhere. Recruiters are partners in this strategy, often seeking out candidates at institutions where high-level turnover is underway since many other members of the senior team will consider making a move. These two approaches—planning to stay and planning to go—are often taken simultaneously as these individuals hedge their bets. And they are wise to do so. Vice presidents who commit to staying on in support of the new president often find themselves encouraged to move on as the new president brings a different vision, finds the old vice president too closely associated with the old regime, brings someone from his or her previous institution, or just finds that the chemistry is not right. Again, the sooner the process for evaluating and making changes is clarified, the better.

As you begin your presidency or vice presidency, especially if this is the first time you have held a position at this level, expect to be both overjoyed and overwhelmed. The thrill of a challenging new opportunity to make a difference in the life of an institution will keep you going. The demands on your time will be limitless, as internal and external audiences seek to get to know you, colleagues bring you important requests and decisions, and you try to deepen your understanding of the institution and the position.

PART II

ADVICE FOR SEARCH COMMITTEES

CHAPTER 9

Understanding the Leadership Opportunity

The search for senior leadership is a critical juncture for an institution. For those who are planning the search, there are several important issues to consider and decisions to make even before the search process is defined and the committee is appointed. The board chair and executive committee, and if possible the full board, should consider these issues in preparation for a presidential search, and the president should consider them before beginning a search for a vice president.

THE REASONS FOR THE SEARCH

Why is this position available? The answer to this question can have a substantial impact on the difficulty and success of the search. If the outgoing president or vice president has left after serving successfully for 10 years and moved to an even more important leadership role in higher education, he or she may leave large shoes to fill, but the vacancy itself will not normally raise concerns in the minds of candidates or the general public. Similarly, there are few concerns if the outgoing person is retiring at a normal age and no rumors are circulating that he or she was forced out.

But if the outgoing person is thought to have been encouraged to leave, or is leaving to take a less desirable position, leaving without another position, leaving after only one or two years, or leaving following a period of controversy, the search will be more difficult. Strong candidates will want to understand the forces that led to the departure, and the board or the president will have to give candidates confidence that the difficulties are not continuing. For example, if a president leaves office because of a micromanaging board, or a CFO leaves because of the president's mismanagement has been blamed on him or her, candidates will stay away. If the faculty and administration have engaged in constant warfare and faculty anger led to a provost's departure, the provost search will probably attract some candidates who are experienced in dealing with or healing conflict, but it will deter other candidates from considering the position, preferring a more productive setting. If the president left because he or she was unable to fulfill the board's expectations for rapid increase in national rankings, but the board has been unwilling to contribute or attract the funds essential for improved rankings, candidates will want clear financial commitments from the board before accepting an offer.

If your institution is faced with a troublesome or even toxic situation that may deter strong candidates, what can you do? The instinct of some boards and presidents is to plunge ahead and hope that the institution's attractive features will outweigh the negatives. Boards may imagine that a bold and skilled leader will be unconcerned about the problems, perhaps even inspired by the challenge. Forging ahead can work. However, when it is combined with unwillingness to reveal the trouble spots or, even worse, with unwillingness to address the underlying problems, it is not a good approach. If the board or president can discuss the difficulties with some candor, then a relationship of mutual respect and trust can be developed with the candidates. If the board or president can say, further, that specific steps have been taken to ameliorate the situation that led to the outgoing person's premature or contentious departure, it is even better.

In some cases, strong candidates will be unwilling to consider a vacancy created by institutional difficulties, and the board must do even more to address the concerns. The board might bring in an organizational consultant to analyze the problems and suggest steps to address them. This approach can assure prospective candidates that the board is aware of the problems, has taken responsibility for dealing with them, and has made progress toward solving them.

Appointing an Interim

Another approach is to appoint an interim person to the position. This allows time to make needed changes. Healing can occur, the situation that caused the toxicity can be changed (making changes in board membership or board policy, for example), and conflicts can be analyzed and addressed. Resuming the search after taking these steps, while it may slow the institution's momentum, may also attract a stronger pool of candidates.

Appointing an interim person before launching a search can be a wise approach in other situations as well. Sometimes the departure of a long-serving president can be jolting for an institution that has experienced limited change during that presidency. Appointing an interim president can accustom the institution to the experience of change and pave the way for a more successful permanent appointment. In other situations, the board of an institution facing a critical decision (e.g., whether a single-sex institution should become coed, or whether a church-related institution should appoint its first lay president) needs to make that decision before selecting a president. In the absence of a decision about coeducation, the search committee will not know whether to seek a new president who supports and is experienced in single-sex education, or who has the skills to lead a transition to coeducation.

Another situation calling for an interim appointment is the president who announces the intention to depart late in the academic year. Rather than launch a hurried search that would lead to the appointment of a new president before the start of the upcoming academic year, the board might appoint an interim president. If the institution's network of potential leaders does not contain someone appropriate to the interim position (e.g., one of the vice presidents, a previous president, a trustee, or a leader in the local community), there are firms that specialize in providing interim institutional leaders. A decision about whether to search quickly or to postpone the search until the following year can depend on many things, such as whether there is a need for a "cooling off period" or a transitional president, and how easy it will be to identify an interim president who can keep up the institutional momentum.

THE COMPENSATION PACKAGE

Once the reasons for the search have been addressed, compensation must be considered. Much has been made of the extraordinarily high salaries of some senior university administrators. Few leaders in higher education administration expect to receive salaries competing with the corporate world. But even so, an exceptionally high salary or other material compensation can get the attention of someone who is otherwise quite content in his or her current position and not seeking to move. Similarly, someone who is earning $300,000 as a dean of business will not normally be interested in a provost position or a presidency that carries a salary of $250,000. Few people are willing to take a cut in pay unless there are other strong countervailing forces, such as an invitation to return to your alma mater, the opportunity to serve a distinctively mission-driven institution, or the wish to move to, or to remain in, an attractive location).

If your institution is able to offer a startlingly attractive salary and compensation package, it will help you to recruit a strong pool of candidates. If the salary is average for your type of institution and location, you can still feel optimistic about attracting strong candidates, but you should anticipate losing a few who are seeking better compensation. If your institution's salaries are below the norm for the position, you have to anticipate a smaller and weaker pool of candidates than you may be hoping for. In this case, the board chair or the president have a responsibility to convey to the search committee that, while aspirations should be high in seeking candidates, there should also be an awareness that some good candidates may be lost because of the below-average compensation, and that other sweeteners should be sought, such as tuition remission for spouse or children, generous study leave or sabbatical, and access to corporate board appointments that could provide supplementary compensation.

LOCATION

Most candidates evaluate a position's salary in the context of comparative cost of living. But this issue tends to attract a candidate's attention more when the cost of living at the new location is *higher* than his or her current location. Candidates will use various Web sites to calculate their current salaries in the context of the new location, and then look for an appropriate increase on top of that. If the cost of living in the new location is *lower* than at the candidate's current location, the candidate is less likely to consider this factor, and in any case will rarely be willing to accept a lower salary.

Cost of living is also an issue for presidents and vice presidents because they in turn must hire others; if the provost, for example, is concerned about the difficulty of recruiting faculty to a region with high housing costs, it may lead to some reluctance to accept the position of provost even though his or her own salary is attractive. Establishment of a program to support housing costs for other faculty and staff members can ease this concern; providing housing support for faculty and for administrators beyond the president is becoming the norm at institutions in San Francisco, Los Angeles, New York, Boston, Miami, and other expensive locations.

Location of the institution is a major factor in recruiting, but not one that can be changed. Still, the board or president should be aware of its impact and consider how the impact might be mitigated or enhanced. Full information about location should be easily available to candidates on the institution's Web site. Candidates may be willing to make the trade-off of taking an attractive position in an unattractive location, but family members may not be as willing; institutions in less attractive locations should make particular efforts to engage the candidate's whole family as they move toward extending an offer. Candidates generally prefer the sunbelt to the snowbelt—especially candidates for senior positions who are generally older and thinking about locations that grandchildren will want to visit or that will be attractive retirement locations once they step down. Some candidates prefer urban locations and some prefer rural locations, but because senior officers tend to travel a great deal, most prefer locations that provide relatively easy access to major airports or highways. There are many outstanding and attractive institutions that are in remote areas or cold climates, or in decaying neighborhoods, that are able to attract outstanding candidates, so this issue should not be considered an unmanageable problem; it is simply one that needs to be addressed and that may cause some candidates not to consider your institution, while others will be attracted to it for the same reason.

INSTITUTIONAL ASPIRATIONS

Institutional ambition is a powerful attraction for candidates. Most institutions seem to crave leadership that can "take us to the next level," and some can even articulate what that means—e.g., to join the prestigious Association of American Universities (AAU), or to move up in the rankings of U.S. *News and World Report*. The energy and enthusiasm that is generated by high institutional aspirations can be compelling for candidates as well as for the institutional community.

But high institutional aspirations can lead to candidate reservations as well. Major upward steps require substantial resources, whether from a capital campaign, increased net tuition revenue, increased extramural support or larger state allocations. Although the board may be energized and the faculty may be determined, an outsider's analysis may be less sanguine, and strong candidates may decline an offer if they doubt that sufficient resources are available to make the great leap forward that the president is expected to lead. Some candidates may doubt the wisdom of an institution's aspiration, wondering whether it will lead to diminished emphasis on teaching or on undergraduate education, or whether it will make a church-related institution more secular. If there is a commitment to institutional ambition, the board should take a very clear-eyed look at what resources and what new approaches or difficult decisions will be necessary to fulfill it. In addition to judging candidates' ability to achieve these goals, boards should evaluate their own capacity as individuals to give or to get the necessary resources, and to evaluate their willingness as a group to make the hard decisions that may be required in order to, for example, increase net tuition revenue (such as a different program mix, some changes in the faculty, or changes in expectations for faculty activities). Is the leap contemplated by the institution achievable? The board's responsibility is to provide a convincing analysis of how the institution plans to achieve its goals, and what the president will have to do in order to accomplish this.

SPAN OF CONTROL

Another element of the position that makes it relatively more or less attractive is span of control. In general, the broader span is more attractive to candidates, and it is more likely to attract experienced candidates—e.g., presidents considering a second presidency, candidates for chief financial officer who have already served as a chief financial officer elsewhere, and so on.

At the vice presidential level, a vice president for finance who has been at an institution that also had a vice president for administration, dividing responsibility for managing the campus, might be eager to move to a setting in which that responsibility is concentrated in the position being filled. A vice president for academic affairs who has had to work in partnership with a CFO may want to move to an executive vice president or senior vice president position to which all other vice presidents report. If the institution has some flexibility on these points, it is worth considering whether the span of control can be increased before the position description is formulated and the search begins. There will certainly be other considerations than simply the desire to attract a stronger candidate pool, but if restructuring is being considered, it should be done before the search.

For presidents, an issue in public institutions may be the presence of a governing board at the campus level. Presidential candidates, especially those who have already been a president, may be attracted to the opportunity to lead an institution with a campus-based board, whose members are not distracted by commitments to support the other institutions in the system. Presidential candidates are unlikely to want to move from an institution with a campus-based board to one with a system-level board. For example, a president who has worked in a public system of higher education in which the board is at the system level rather than the campus level (e.g., Wisconsin) may be eager to move to a presidency in a public system in which the campus has its own governing board (e.g., New Jersey). There are hybrid models as well, in which there is a campus board with specified responsibilities but not the full range of fiduciary responsibilities (e.g., Pennsylvania).

INTERNAL CANDIDATES

The presence of internal candidates is worth considering at an early stage in the search process. While this factor is not fully controllable, and in fact the board or the president may not know if there will be internal candidates, some good guesses can be made. If an interim president or vice president has been appointed, decide whether that person will be permitted to be a candidate and, if so, whether he or she is inclined to be a candidate. Sometimes interim appointees initially say that they are not interested in the permanent appointment, but having had a taste of the role, they decide they want to stay on for a longer term.

If there is a strong feeling that an outsider is needed in order to bring new blood, or to balance other longtime internal members of the senior team, or to avoid the political complexities of an internal appointment, it may be best to state that at the beginning of the search. This can avoid the difficult situation of later having to turn down and potentially offend an internal candidate who may be a highly valued member of the community but not a good fit for the position. Whether or not this is appropriate will depend on the details of the situation. Before ruling out internal candidates, consider the possibility that circumstances may change during the course of the search and the president or board may wish to appoint an internal candidate; if internal candidates have been ruled out in advance, this will be much more awkward.

If there is a strong internal candidate, and particularly if that person is serving in an interim capacity, or if he or she has been second in line to the vacant position (for instance, the executive vice president in a presidential search, or the dean of students in a search for chief student affairs officer), it is highly likely that potential outside candidates will be aware of this and, as a result, may be discouraged from applying. Sometimes outside candidates know the internal candidates personally and are reluctant to compete with them because of friendship. Sometimes potential candidates know how capable the internal candidates are—or how highly favored they are within the institution—and may be unwilling to compete with them because the odds of being selected are reduced. In fact, when announcing an interim appointment, an unusually enthusiastic press release posted on the Web site can be the signal to potential external candidates that applying is both risky and a waste of time.

Some searches have "quasi-internal" candidates—the person who used to be at the institution and moved on, the alumnus, or the member of the board. Any of these can be potentially strong candidates, perceived to bring deep knowledge of and commitment to the institution, while also bringing familiarity with a larger world and a greater range of institutional solutions by virtue of having worked elsewhere. At the same time, each of these candidates can have heavy baggage. The former employee who moved elsewhere may be remembered fondly by some, but negatively by others. The political climate may have changed since this person left, and his or her supporters may not be in a position to influence the selection process. The alumnus may be seen as limited by his or her particular student experience. The trustee may have made difficult and unpopular decisions that would taint a candidacy. Candidates in this quasi-internal group typically get feedback that lacks insight, candor, or both; they are often encouraged because they are valued members of the community, or close personal friends, but in fact they may not stand a chance as a candidate. These situations should be handled with particular sensitivity.

Why would an institution hold a search if there is an internal candidate who is very strong? Some would argue—especially those with experience in the corporate world, where succession planning is a normal practice—that the interim vice president or interim president, having been tested in other roles in the institution, should simply be appointed without a search. An evaluation process might occur in which the readiness and fit of the internal candidate is tested, but a full-blown search, with the cost in both time and money, can be avoided. Some have advocated for this approach in higher education.[1]

But there are reasons why most institutions carry out searches even when an internal candidate is strongly preferred from the start. For example, if the senior team is homogeneous, lacking in women or people of color, a search is an opportunity to bring some diversity into the administration. If there are multiple internal candidates, a search provides a systematic process of evaluation and comparison. If there is a full national search, the person appointed will have been tested against that national standard; and if he or she is still found to be the best candidate, his or her legitimacy will be enhanced as a result (although the pool against which the testing occurs may be somewhat weaker than it would otherwise have been). On balance, most institutions consider the options and decide to hold a full search for senior leadership positions, even when they are fairly certain to appoint someone from inside.

ANNOUNCING THE SEARCH

Once the board or the president has thought through these issues, an announcement should be made. Typically, the announcement of a presidential search will be broader than the announcement of a vice presidential search, going out to alumni, community members, foundation leaders, and all interested publics. If there has been time to address the issues of the interim appointment, organizational structure, committee membership, and possible search consultant, those items can be addressed in the initial announcement of the vacancy. For example, "We are pleased that our board chair has agreed to serve as interim president next year, during our presidential search. She has told us that she will not be a candidate for the position. We will be supported in carrying out our full national search by _____ of _____ Executive Search. The following individuals have agreed to serve on the search committee." Or, "I have decided to make some organizational changes that will considerably strengthen the role of the provost. I believe that this will substantially enhance the attractiveness of the position and our ability to attract strong candidates."

Announcing the selection of a search consultant, or the process that will lead to the selection, can signal the seriousness with which the search is viewed. Announcing the members of the search committee can signal how inclusive the search will be, can show that the most respected members of the community have been selected, and—most importantly—can show that the next step in the process of succession has already been taken. The next chapter focuses on the issues surrounding search committees. The value of providing all these elements in the initial announcement is sending the message, "We have dealt with all the difficult issues of transition and there will be no instability." The risk, of course, is that various constituencies or individuals may ask, "Why did you make all these decisions without consulting us?"

NOTES

1. Lucie Lapovsky, "The Best-Laid Succession Plans," *Trusteeship* (Jan.–Feb. 2006), 20–24.

CHAPTER 10

Assembling
Strong Search Committees

The attractiveness of the institution and the position are the most powerful factors in shaping the strength of the candidate pool. The next most important factor is the quality of the search committee. The membership of the committee sends a powerful signal to candidates about the institution's values and aspirations. A committee and its chair should be respected members of the institutional community who have good judgment and a clear understanding of the nature and needs of the position. They should also be individuals who are willing and able to work hard and are disciplined and well organized, who put institution-wide priorities before narrower interests, who are able to maintain confidentiality during the search and forever after, and who are able to present the institution to candidates in a manner that is both engaging and candid. Following are some more detailed observations about the characteristics most valuable in search committee members.

CHARACTERISTICS OF
GOOD SEARCH COMMITTEE MEMBERS
Good Judgment and the Respect of the Community

Search committee members, and especially the chair of the committee, above all should have good judgment. They will have a vast number of decisions to make, both large and small, at times of crisis and at ordinary times. Their decisions will shape the position criteria and the advertisement, the tone of the preliminary interviews and the questions asked of candidates, the participation of various groups and individuals in the second round of interviews, the confidentiality of the search process, and of course the selection of candidates. If there are points at which the search is jeopardized by candidate withdrawals, breaches of confidentiality, conflicts among search committee members, or campus crises outside the scope of the search, the committee will have to bring its best collective judgment to bear. Seek individuals who have the respect of their colleagues; this kind of appointment can significantly enhance the stature of the committee and its ability to attract strong candidates.

Understanding of the Position

All search committee members should have at least some understanding of the nature of the position being filled. All may need to round out their understanding, but they should begin with a general sense of the organizational unit (e.g., some understanding of enrollment issues if the search is for the chief enrollment management officer) and the issues it is facing. Some will be more aware of undergraduate or of graduate issues, some will grasp financial aid complexities, some will have an understanding of the overlap between enrollment and advancement—but all should come with some knowledge they can share with others on the committee, as well as an awareness that they may not fully understand the position and an openness to learning more. Committee members with little grasp of the position will not do a good job of representing the opportunity to candidates, and they take up a seat on the committee that could go to someone better able to make this contribution to recruiting. Committee members should also grasp the intentions of the appointing officer; a committee seeking presidential candidates who will be fundamentally unsatisfactory to the board will be wasting everyone's time. A board that wants to appoint a president who is primarily a fund-raiser should be cautious about appointing a committee whose members are focused on academic pedigree or internal management skills to the exclusion of capacity to build external relationships. If that is the committee's approach, a strong orientation conversation might help to set the process on the right track—or might persuade the board to rethink its expectations.

Time

The ability to invest time in the search process is essential. The process takes a lot of time over a period of four to six months. The planning process requires reading, thinking, and committee discussion. The review of candidates requires a great deal of time for reading and rereading the often voluminous candidate files. Preliminary interviews can require setting aside two full days in the midst of many other obligations. Second-round interviews and the gathering of feedback from colleagues, as well as analyzing that feedback with other committee members, can require considerable time and effort. Final deliberations can be brisk, but they may also be protracted. Committee members and the committee chair should be able to devote the necessary time to the search process, and should be willing to trust the judgment of others on the committee if they must miss a meeting. Individuals who plan to be away from campus for substantial periods during the time of the search, or who are not available during the normal workday or during many days of the week, may not be the best ones to appoint to the committee.

On the other hand, do not appoint committee members simply because they have a lot of time. Those who are not busy may not be the most respected members of the community, and their appointment can undermine respect for the process and the outcome.

Institutional Perspective and Teamwork

Most search committee members have, in some sense, a constituency to represent. They may be trustees, or managers in a certain area of the institution (academic, financial, advancement, student affairs, etc.), or faculty in a particular division, or staff with a certain location in the institutional hierarchy, or graduate or undergraduate students, and so on. They should be able to express the concerns and represent the views of those constituencies. But they should also be able to see the institution as a whole, with overarching needs and with institutional priorities that may not necessarily be consistent with the priorities of their constituency. In committee meetings, these individuals need to become a team that supports the institution overall.

One of the most common examples of discrepant perspectives across institutional sectors is the faculty who seek presidential candidates who can provide academic vision and leadership, and the trustees who seek a strong external presence and fund-raising ability. In the ideal committee, the trustees on the committee understand (or come to understand) that the academic mission is central to the institution and that the new president or vice president must be fully committed to and able to represent and support that mission. Simultaneously, the faculty on the committee understand (or come to understand) that without a strong external presence and fund-raising ability, the academic goals can not be accomplished—or, as they say, "no money, no mission." The ideal committee chair has the skills to create a sense of mutual understanding, institutional perspective, and teamwork.

Confidentiality

Committee members can be certain that, unless they are somehow sequestered during the search, they will feel pressure to divulge confidential information. Breaches of confidentiality can seriously damage a search, and can cause candidates to decline or withdraw, losing candidates who may be among the strongest. Those who do not withdraw from this particular search may be badly burned by the experience and lose confidence in the confidentiality of searches at other institutions. The credibility of the institution and the search committee are damaged if confidentiality is breached.

When there is a leak from a search committee, fingers are often pointed at students. But I find that more often, trustees are at fault. They have what they think are confidential conversations with friends at a cocktail party and discover that their friends talk to other friends and what they confided is soon widely known. Staff and faculty are often pressed for information by colleagues who begin with innocent questions ("So, how is the search going?") and progress subtly toward information about particular candidates ("So, is Jane Smith a candidate?"); committee members who do not immediately end the conversation are likely to find themselves saying more than they intended. Another hazard is the political allegiance that committee members may have toward campus groups; if the candidate who is the preferred choice of the union or of the faculty or student governance group does not become a finalist, a disgruntled committee member may pass along insider information and generate controversy that can seriously damage a search.

It is impossible to know in advance who will breach confidentiality through carelessness or while under pressure, but there are certainly some people who are known to routinely trade information for friendship or for influence; these people should not be appointed to search committees. If such individuals are appointed, the chair needs to talk with them directly to remind them of the importance of confidentiality. Some committees ask every member to sign a written statement before the search begins, affirming that they will not divulge confidential information. While they have no legal standing, such statements do serve as a formal reminder. (See Appendix E for a sample code of ethics for search committees.) Other committees place an item on every meeting agenda that asks committee members to report all conversations that they have had about the search with non–committee members since the last meeting; such a request creates considerable interpersonal pressure not to discuss the search.

There are other ways of breaching confidentiality. The deliberations about candidates always include exploration of both strengths and weaknesses, and even after a candidate is appointed, revealing what was said and who said it can be damaging to the appointee or to the committee member who is reported to have spoken against the candidate. It is especially important not to reveal whether the person appointed was the first choice or the last choice of the search committee or of particular constituencies. This information has potential to weaken the appointee's effectiveness in the position. Particularly when an internal candidate is involved, extensive information is reviewed in committee discussion and grievances are aired that have accumulated over the years against even the most popular administrator. This candor is an important element in the review of candidates, but it will be lacking unless committee members are confident that confidentiality will be maintained.

A prime venue for breaches of confidentiality is subsequent search committees at the same institution. People involved in the presidential search who serve on subsequent vice presidential search committees, for example, are particularly likely to reveal the deliberations of the earlier committee. These individuals may have the illusion that the open discussion of one committee is transposed into the next search. Since participation in subsequent search committees provides a setting in which confidentiality is especially at risk, the chair of such a committee should express appreciation for the understanding of the search process that experienced committee members bring. But the chair should also remind participants that there will be no discussion of the individual candidates involved in that search, and particularly the candidate who was ultimately appointed. The only exception to this general principle is that a committee should be aware that a vice presidential candidate was an unsuccessful presidential candidate. This information does not necessarily make the vice presidential candidacy fatally flawed, but it would be awkward for the second committee not to be aware of what the first committee had decided and the information upon which their decision was based.

Capacity to Attract Candidates

Committee members are often the first and most substantial points of contact between the candidate and the institution. Apart from internal and quasi-internal candidates, many candidates have little substantive knowledge of the institution that is searching. Even the consultant who may represent the institution is not personally part of it. A positive conversation during the search committee's preliminary interview can attract a candidate (leading many to say, "I'm even more interested in this position now that I've met the search committee"). It can also turn off a candidate. I have had the experience of calling a candidate after the preliminary interview to tell her that she had been selected to move ahead in the search process, only to have her say that she did not think there was good chemistry with the committee, which seemed to dismiss her ideas or to lack enthusiasm for the institution. The personal qualities and institutional loyalty of committee members, their grasp of the position and its issues, and their ability to convey institutional aspirations, make a major contribution to attracting strong candidates.

Diversity

The committee overall should be diverse. A committee composed solely of white men may be less likely to attract and select candidates who are women or people of color. Those candidates look around the interview table and find it difficult to believe claims that diversity is valued. In institutions that lack diversity in the administration, staff, and faculty, the few women and people of color who might serve on executive search committees may already be stretched thin by the demands of other committees seeking diverse membership. Nonetheless, diversifying presidential and vice presidential search committees is an investment in further diversifying the campus.

SELECTION OF A COMMITTEE CHAIR

Selection of the chair of the search committee is also a critical element. The chair must have all the characteristics of good committee members, as well as leadership qualities. The chair needs to build the disparate committee members into a team, create a committee culture, and move the search toward a successful conclusion. This is especially true if the committee decides to work without a search consultant.

Team-Building

The ideal search committee recognizes the constituencies that members represent, while also supporting broader institutional goals. The chair of the search committee should be able to articulate the need for this balance to the committee by talking about it, and by modeling the balance in his or her own behavior.

Leadership in Creating a Culture

The committee chair takes the lead in creating a culture in the committee. It should be a culture of mutual respect, in which all voices are heard and varied opinions are respected. The loud or charismatic voices of one or two members should not be permitted to capture the uncritical support of others, swamping the voices of minority opinions or of those who are less outspoken or articulate. This can sometimes call for considerable diplomacy, including at times taking aside those who are suppressing the voices of others, dealing with irreconcilable differences between committee members, and easing thorny personal relationships. It can call for infinite patience, as the committee takes the time to listen to everyone. Leadership can call for decisiveness, as the chair asks for a vote to clarify the results of an endless debate, or puts a proposal on the table that offers a way out of a morass. There is no single leadership style that works best. I have seen exceptionally effective chairs who insist that every last thought of every last committee member be heard before a decision is made, and I have seen exceptionally effective chairs who rule out of order any comment that echoes a comment already made.

Ability to Reach a Conclusion

Even the most smoothly functioning committee can be challenged by the need to make a final recommendation of the one candidate to be offered the position, or by the need to rank the candidates. A chair who is asked to lead the committee through this step should try to build consensus in the committee before calling for a vote. Ideally, all participants will support the conclusion. Even if they do not, there should be a final vote in which there is unanimous support for the candidate who is the choice of the majority. The chair should describe the need for this unanimous affirmation of support at the start of the search. While it is not essential, it has great value in providing a public statement of support for the candidate as his or her appointment begins.

There are some committees that do not vote. The institutional culture may prefer consensus over voting. Or, the chair or the appointing officer may specify that there will be no voting to make it clear that the committee is not making the selection. Even in these situations, the chair will need to exert leadership to move deliberations along and bring them to a close.

The committee should not seek consensus at the expense of quality. A consensus candidate can often be the lowest common denominator—the candidate who is sufficiently bland to have avoided offending anyone. The chair who recognizes this risk can articulate it and provide a rationale for selecting the stronger candidate in spite of some opposition, and at the same time offer recognition and reassurance to those whose preferred candidate is not selected.

MAKING APPOINTMENTS TO THE SEARCH COMMITTEE

With these criteria in mind for the chair and committee members, who makes committee appointments? Often this is a matter of institutional policy, which may call for a Noah's ark of members—five trustees, four faculty, three staff, two students, one alumnus, etc. Policy may also dictate the manner of selection—e.g., trustees selected by the executive committee, or faculty elected by their peers. Established policies should be respected but can often make it difficult to achieve the goals described above while simultaneously appointing a balanced group that includes men and women, majority and minority group members, and representatives of the major units within the institution.

If there is a single appointing authority, achieving the goals described above is more likely. The best committees are created when the constituencies provide slates of names from which the appointing authority can select a skilled and diverse group. If the authority to appoint committee members is dispersed, or if committee members are elected, it can be useful to provide a summary of the expectations described above so that participants in the committee selection process can reflect on who would be best suited to serve. If the president or the board has appointing authority for some subgroup of the committee, they might defer their appointments until the others are made so that they can take into account any missing elements in the group.

SIZE OF THE COMMITTEE

The size of the search committee is a compelling issue for many board chairs and presidents. But within limits, I believe that size should be seen as a relatively minor concern. Committees with more than 20 members can be difficult to manage, but few committees are that large. The difference between 10 and 15 is not significant. If fulfilling other needs results in adding a few more people, that should not be defined as an insurmountable problem.

Some vice presidential searches have no search committee or virtually none; the president may, for example, select a vice president for advancement by working directly with a search consultant, only bringing in a small group of colleagues (trustees, other vice presidents) for a second round of interviews to provide broader insights and thus help to narrow the field from three, four, or five candidates down to the one to be selected. This advisory group can also help to recruit the candidates by showing their enthusiasm for the institution, talking about what a privilege it is to work with this president, and analyzing the challenges for the institution from their varied perspectives. A search committee of one with an advisory group is very different from the more typical committee of a dozen or so. A committee of one typically allows a search to move more quickly and removes all ambiguity about who has responsibility for selection. But there are few situations in which such a limited range of involvement in a search is feasible, and the advantages of a streamlined committee do not exceed the advantages of the inclusive process that is the norm in higher education.

THE CHARGE TO THE SEARCH COMMITTEE

Structuring the typical presidential search committee requires first determining the charge to the committee. If the committee is charged with actually selecting the single preferred candidate (even though it may be ratified by a vote of the board), or charged with rank-ordering the finalists, then members of the board of trustees must dominate the committee. This is because the responsibility to appoint the president cannot be delegated by the board. If board members are not the dominant group on the committee, the board will have given up its most fundamental responsibility. In this situation, there might be, for example, six trustees and a total of five others (faculty, staff, students, administrators, etc.). If adequate representation of those other constituencies requires eight non-trustee committee members, then there should be at least nine trustees; this drives up the total size of the committee, but as I have said, I believe that is a less important consideration. The more important issue is the need for the board to dominate the selection of the new president. The board chair should not be reluctant to specify that this is the reason for the numerical dominance of board members on the committee.

If, on the other hand, the committee is charged with bringing to the board a group of three to five candidates, unranked, the constraints on committee composition are changed. The trustees do not have to dominate the committee because, in the end, the full board (or a committee of the board) will make the selection. It is true that other constituencies can shape the list of three to five finalists, but that carries less risk for the board's authority. There should certainly be several trustees, but their total number does not have to exceed the total number of other members. In this case, the focus is typically on how many faculty should come from each academic division, whether there should be the same number of faculty as staff, whether there should be both an undergraduate and a graduate student and perhaps a continuing education student as well, whether a single individual can represent both the alumni and the community, and so on. There is no formula for success; each institution will need to decide what is most in keeping with its culture and politics.

As part of charging the search committee, some boards and presidents ask members to sign a code of ethics that commits them to maintaining confidentiality and adhering to ethical standards and best practices. A sample code of ethics is included in Appendix E.

Some committees are challenged by various campus voices even before they begin work. Common reasons for such challenges are the lack of ethnic diversity, the lack of representation of a particular organizational segment (e.g., no member of a science department, no graduate student, no member of a collective bargaining group), or the disproportionate representation of segments (e.g., more faculty than staff). Some chairs or appointing officers dig in their heels and decline to address these concerns. While that may be the right decision, it is sometimes made for the wrong reason—concern about size. Whether the committee has 10 or 12 or 14 people is of little consequence. Many committees of 18 or 20 can function smoothly, and I have worked with a committee of over 40 people (although I do not recommend that!). Inclusiveness is more important than keeping the committee small.

In the midst of the debate and even controversy that can sometimes surround the appointment of presidential and vice presidential search committees, it is important to remember that a smoothly functioning committee can be an excellent occasion for finding common ground and building relationships and mutual understanding across sectors (e.g., faculty and trustees). The members of many presidential search committees observe once the process ends that the search was a wonderful and rare opportunity to get to know and understand each other.

CHAPTER 11

What Search Consultants Do

At the start of a presidential search, the board has many important issues to address. One of the most important is whether or not it will appoint a consultant to assist with a presidential search. In a vice presidential search, the president must also consider whether to use a consultant.

WHAT DO SEARCH CONSULTANTS DO?

Most people think that the consultant's most important contribution is the development of a strong and diverse pool of candidates, bringing into the pool individuals who would not have entered the search if they had not been recruited. This is the most prominent contribution that consultants make, but not the only one. Broadly speaking, the consultant can:

- Provide an appraisal of how the position and the institution will be viewed by potential candidates, and offer advice about how to highlight strengths and deal with limitations;
- Advise on the composition of the search committee and its charge;
- Provide leadership for the search process to the degree that the search chair wishes to delegate it;
- Suggest best practices at every step in the process and guidance about the consequences of taking various approaches;
- Gather opinions from all constituencies and provide a draft position specification that analyzes institutional issues and opportunities;
- Formulate and execute a recruiting plan tailored to the institution and the position, ultimately building a strong pool of candidates;
- Screen candidates and present a slate for committee review;
- Carry out reference checks and gather background information;
- Assist in the process of extending an offer and negotiations with the selected candidate;
- Notify candidates who are no longer under consideration.

The search committee may be able to carry out all these tasks without a consultant; and even with a consultant, committee members may have to be active in some of these tasks, such as recruiting the strongest candidates. But the tasks are time consuming (e.g., phone calls to recruit candidates), and they can require considerable project management (e.g., establishing a database to track progress of each candidate through the process, from the point of nomination, through interviews, to the point of appointment or being dropped from further consideration). They also require some skill and familiarity with higher education (e.g., formulating a recruiting strategy). Without a consultant, the search chair will have to manage all these tasks or identify people to whom the tasks can be delegated. If the tasks are delegated to staff, their normal responsibilities may have to be put aside. I know of no calculation of the cost of carrying out a search without a search consultant. Each institution will have to assess its own capacity to cover the cost of a consultant or to absorb the work of the search.

In addition to the value of the consultant to the institution, there is also a value to the candidates, which has indirect benefits for the institution. Candidates often report that they find it easier to navigate the search process with a consultant, and as a result they may be more inclined to actually become candidates. If they are familiar with the consultant, they may be more inclined to make an initial exploratory contact. As described in Part I, consultants can provide candidates with feedback and advice about whether to enter the search, and about how best to present themselves on paper and in interviews. They can also give candidates a relatively objective appraisal of the institution. They can give strategic advice as the search proceeds, and keep candidates posted about the progress of the search and the meaning of delays and other schedule changes. The care and feeding of candidates is a very important but time-consuming part of the search process, and in some ways the care of the candidates *not* selected is even more important than the care of the winner; the candidates not selected are receiving bad news, but even so they should leave the process feeling well cared for and with enhanced respect for the institution, even though the outcome was not what they had hoped for. Search committee chairs can play an important role in relation to candidates by phoning them at key points in the search, but that responsibility is more optional and less onerous if it is shared with the consultant.

Using a consultant does not guarantee, however, that all your candidates will leave your search process in a happy frame of mind. General feedback from candidates about their experience in various searches and with various consultants suggests that feeling ill-treated in a search is probably the major complaint that candidates have about searches. As one might expect, this is particularly true of those who are not selected. Consultants typically strive to treat candidates with respect, but even when consultants are involved, candidates may complain that they did not have sufficient contact with the consultant, were not kept informed about the progress of the search, were not given helpful feedback, or were initially encouraged but then dropped without explanation. Some of these complaints have merit. Often candidates who do not get the position they were seeking are understandably unhappy and may blame that on the consultant. Some candidates have unrealistic expectations about the frequency of the contacts and nature of the attention they will receive, sometimes as a function of their belief that they are a stronger candidate than they actually are. Search consultants try to address these concerns and to give candidates realistic expectations (with this book, of course, serving as an effort in that direction). Sometimes they fall short of this goal.

SHOULD YOU USE A SEARCH CONSULTANT?

I want to be clear about the perspective that I bring to the question of using search consultants. When I was in institutional leadership positions, before becoming a search consultant, I virtually never used a consultant's services, and some of the searches I participated in were very successful. Today, having seen what a consultant can provide, I believe that consultants increase the likelihood of a successful search process and outcome. But many senior leadership searches are successful without consulting support, and one goal of this book is to provide guidance for search committees working without consultants. I will lay out in some detail the approach taken by search consultants, enabling the search committee to replicate those approaches on its own. At the same time, committees that are using consultants will find it helpful to understand how consultants work so that they can work more effectively with the one they have selected.

Although many institutions use consultants to support their presidential and vice presidential searches, there are some situations in which using a search consultant may not be as important:[1]

- Institutions that are very well known and highly regarded, and in desirable locations, may be able to attract outstanding candidates without much effort.

- Institutions that are at the very top of their sectors (e.g., Harvard among private universities, Swarthmore among private colleges) can focus their recruiting on a small number of peer institutions. It is likely that the majority of prospective candidates are easily identifiable by the search committee at the start of the process, or may even be known to them personally.

- When there is a single very strong internal candidate, it may not be necessary to invest in a search consultant. The consultant's ability to attract strong candidates from outside the institution will be especially limited if the presence of an internal heir apparent is well known, further reducing the value of the consultant's contribution.

- When a church-related institution seeks a member of the clergy for a leadership role, there may be enough knowledge of potential candidates within the institution or within the religious community that outside consultants are not needed.

- When diversity is already present in the senior leadership team, it may be easier to attract a diverse pool of candidates without consultant support.

Some institutions may not be able to afford the cost of a consultant. Although the risk of an unsuccessful search is also costly, both monetarily and in lost credibility, time, and momentum, it may still be necessary to take that risk.

As a consultant, I have seen many search committees flounder when they work on their own, and I have been called in to support many searches that were initially carried out without consultant support but could not be successfully concluded. Certainly there are cases in which consultant-supported searches have to be extended for lack of the right candidates, and cases in which the person appointed turns out not to be a good fit. If the search has to be extended because it has not concluded with an appointment, you will normally not have to pay any additional fee to the consulting firm. If the person appointed is unsuccessful, there may be a guarantee in your contract with the search firm, specifying the conditions under which the firm will redo the search without an additional fee. In most cases, I believe that the investment in a search consultant is a good one.

Some search committees, seeking to reduce costs or believing that most of the tasks of the search can be handled internally, wonder if it is possible to hire a search firm to build the candidate pool but not to handle the rest of the search-related tasks. Most search firms will not agree solely to build the pool, although smaller firms may do it. But before you take this approach, consider the full array of support that a consultant can provide and be sure that you would not actually benefit from that as well.

SELECTING A SEARCH CONSULTANT

If you decide that you do want to use a consultant, your next task is to select a search firm. There are many resources available to assist you.

- Look at the *Chronicle of Higher Education* advertisements for positions like the one you are filling. See which firms are supporting institutions that are like yours in some way—located in your region, similar in type (public, private, church-related, two-year), similar in mission (with a focus on research or teaching, for example), or similar in stature and character (members of the Association of American Universities, or the American Association of State Colleges and Universities, or the Ivy League).

- Talk to your counterparts at institutions that have recently conducted searches for presidents or vice presidents. Ask them what it was like to work with the firm they selected, and ask for their appraisal of the particular consultants and support staff with whom they worked. Remember, though, that every institution and the personalities of participants are different, so a good fit for another institution may not be a good fit for you, and vice versa.

- Use the *Presidential Search Guidelines and Directory* published by the Association of Governing Boards (AGB).[2] Updated every few years, the 2005 edition includes profiles of 16 search firms, as well as detailed suggestions about how to carry out the process of selecting a consultant.

- Invite a selected group of firms to submit proposals to carry out your search. After screening the written proposals, invite a few firms to make presentations to your search committee, either in person or by phone or videoconference. Before you make a selection, talk to references, just as you will before you hire the new president or vice president.

Once you have gathered all this information and need to make a final selection, what should you be looking for? Several areas are important to consider:

- *Expertise with your type of institution:* Most searches look for candidates who have experience in institutions of roughly similar size, type, and stature. There are certainly many contrary examples, but you want your search consultant to be familiar with the world in which you are functioning (e.g., large research universities, small private colleges, two-year institutions) and with the people who are leaders or emerging leaders in those institutions. The consultant who brings this familiarity and this network will get a faster start and will be able to avoid pursuing candidates who have fatal flaws because they became aware of those flaws when working with these candidates in previous searches. Instead, they will be able to focus quickly on the best prospects, and their prior relationships will help them to get the attention of these strong candidates.

  Some consultants not only have general expertise with your type of institution; they also have specific knowledge of your institution. You may have retained this firm to work on your presidential search and now you are considering using the firm again in your search for a new chief advancement officer. Or, you may have used the consultant in a CFO search and now want to consider using him or her for the presidential search. In either case, the consultant has the advantage of already knowing the institution and its issues, some of the key players, and the approach you want to take in the search. But there can be a downside as well; a consultant who worked with your institution a few years ago may not be as open to seeing the changes in the strategic plan, in the financial health, or in the culture of the institution since that time. You will need to decide whether familiarity or freshness is more valuable to you at this time.

  There is a hazard, too, to using the search firm that has a great deal of experience working with institutions like yours. The hazard is that the firm must declare a great many institutions to be "off limits" to their recruiting efforts. (Off-limits restrictions are discussed in greater detail below.) If the firm has worked with an institution within the previous year, those institutions will normally be off limits to recruiting for a year after the search is completed. So the value of the firm's familiarity with these institutions has to be balanced against the disadvantage of these recruiting limitations.

  Another risk when using a firm that has extensive experience with your type of institution is that they will be working simultaneously with competing searches. If you are concerned about a potential conflict of interest in this situation, ask the consultant whether he or she is currently working with a peer institution, or anticipates doing that in the course of your search, and consider how the consultant anticipates handling possible candidate overlap.

- *Capacity to carry out the work in a reasonable period of time:* You need to know whether your expectations for the search timetable are reasonable. Many institutions would like to complete their searches in a month or two. This may be possible in some situations, but they are rare, and the expectation of such a rapid process is probably not realistic. If you set an aggressive timetable, you should expect that some firms will decline to submit proposals, or their proposals will include a caveat about the schedule. This is normally because consultants have prior commitments that preclude allocating extensive time to your search.

But if your timetable is realistic (e.g., four to six months), you should be sure that the consultant has the capacity to carry out the search. You should not expect that yours will be the only search the consultant is supporting, but you do need to know that he or she has enough scheduling flexibility that you will be able to get started and to keep the process moving without scheduling conflicts caused by the consultant's overbooked calendar. Naturally it is important to set the meeting schedule in consultation with the consultant so that mutually workable dates can be set.

- *Personal sense of comfort and fit:* You will be spending hours of meetings over many months with the consultant you select. You need to be sure that the person you meet in the consultant selection process is the person you will actually be working with, and that the search chair and the committee are comfortable both with the consultant's tone and style and with the approach that the consultant plans to take with your search. Remember too that the consultant will be the face of your institution to the candidates; you should be comfortable with the way that he or she will represent you.

VARIATION IN CONSULTANT APPROACHES

Firms differ in their approach to searches, and individual consultants within a firm may differ too. Some firms take an approach typically used in corporate searches. They will bring you the individuals the consultants consider to be the five or 10 best candidates for the position, and you will have the opportunity to interview these candidates and select the one you prefer.

Other firms take a nondirective view of the candidate pool. They will bring you the files of all the candidates who apply as well as the candidates they have recruited, and the consultant may give you relatively little guidance as to which candidates he or she thinks are the best fit. The search committee will have the opportunity—or the burden!—of selecting the best on its own.

And, of course, there are firms that take the middle ground, allowing the committee to review all the candidates who emerged through the process but also letting you know which candidates they view as the best fit for the position, and the information upon which they base this judgment.

Another area of difference to consider in selecting a search consultant is the amount of attention you and the candidates will get from the consultant. Some consultants are very involved, will attend virtually every meeting of the search committee, will be easily available to talk to the search chair as needed (including evenings and weekends), and will respond instantly to your e-mails from a handheld computer. Some consultants have a workload that will not allow them to be so available, or a style that makes them disinclined to be so involved, but the quality of their work or their reputation may justify the more limited access.

Consultant involvement with candidates differs as well. Some consultants stay in very close touch with candidates, especially those who appear best suited to your position, keeping them updated about the search process, and preparing them for each step along the way. Others take a more hands-off approach, perhaps allowing more room for the search chair to build a relationship with the candidates.

COSTS OF SEARCH CONSULTANTS

While the style and approach of search consultants differ, the cost of using a search consultant does not differ very much across search firms. There is a relatively standard approach to cost: the professional fee is typically one-third of the first year's salary for the position being filled, and normally you will be asked to cover both general overhead expenses (phone, fax, mailings, etc.) and specific expenses such as advertising and travel for candidates and for consultants.

Focusing first on the fee, you will want to clarify exactly what is considered as part of the salary for purposes of calculating the fee; for example, is a bonus included, or a housing allowance, or a salary that might be paid to the president's spouse? You also need to know whether there is a minimum fee. If you are hiring a vice president who will be paid $150,000 a year, you might expect the fee to be $50,000. The firm, however, may have a minimum fee of $60,000.

Different firms handle expenses differently; for example, some firms bundle the overhead expenses into the fee, and some will bill you for those expenses separately. The total for all these costs can be substantial, but remember that most of the major expenses (apart from the fee and the cost of the consultant's travel) will be incurred regardless of whether or not you use a consultant—you will still advertise, you will still have candidates traveling to interviews, and so on. If you are comparing the costs of using a consultant with the costs of carrying out the search on your own, keep these factors in mind.

PROVISIONS OF CONSULTANT CONTRACTS
The Guarantee

In addition to fees and expenses, there are several other key items in your agreement with the search consultant. Many search firms offer a guarantee, typically for one year. This means that, if the person appointed to the position as a result of this search leaves the position within one year for certain specified reasons, the firm will redo the search without an additional fee. Normally this guarantee would not apply if the person appointed becomes seriously ill or dies, or if his or her personal situation changes (e.g., marrying someone in a distant location and deciding to move away, or moving to care for an aging parent). Rather, you are being protected against a lack of fit that suggests a poor choice. If the person appointed leaves the position within one year for professional reasons, the guarantee normally would apply.

Off-Limits Agreements

The contract with the search firm normally contains some kind of off-limits agreement. This is a two-edged sword. On the one hand, the off-limits agreement protects your institution and especially the person appointed through this search from the firm's recruiting efforts on behalf of other clients. Consider, for example, that your institution is a large and prominent research university included among the members of the Association of American Universities (AAU). You use a particular consulting firm to help you identify a new academic vice president. It is likely that the firm will, in the next year or two, be asked to assist a search for president at one of your peer institutions in the AAU. The off-limits policy assures you that your relatively new vice president will not be recruited *by that firm* for that position for a certain period of time (obviously this person can still be recruited by other firms). You should determine the period of time when your appointee is off limits; three years would be a typical period of restriction.

There is also some protection for others at your institution. For example, if you use a consultant to assist with a presidential search, many firms will consider that all the president's direct reports are off limits to recruiting for one year. This assures that the new president's team will not be dismantled in the first year. This can be a significant protection. Many senior officers of a university with a new president are interested in exploring other opportunities, since they can not be certain that there will be a good fit between their skills and style and the expectations of the new person. Or the new president may simply want to have his or her own team, so it makes good sense for a vice president to consider other options. Typically there is a mechanism for supporting a vice president who wants to look elsewhere within this one-year period; the off-limits agreement may allow candidates to be recruited and to become involved in another search if they notify the person to whom they report and obtain their agreement. The scope of the off-limits agreement varies among search firms; at one extreme, some firms protect everyone working at the institution, and at the other extreme, some firms protect only the direct reports to the position being filled. Clarify the limits of the off-limits agreement with the firm you select.

Off-limits agreements can also have a downside for the client institution. For example, if you are at an AAU institution that is looking for a president, and you retain a search firm that has worked with peer institutions in the past year, the individuals whom they placed at those institutions, and the leadership teams reporting to those individuals, may be off limits to recruiting by that firm. This can limit your access to some of the candidates in whom you have the greatest interest. You may wish that the consultant could overlook the agreement with the other institutions, but ultimately it is a feature that serves you well; a consultant who respects the off-limits agreement in support of your search may one day be more likely to respect the off-limits agreement with your institution in support of a search elsewhere.

NOTES

1. Jean A. Dowdall, "When Colleges Should, and Should Not, Use Executive Search Firms," in James Martin and James E. Samels & Associates, *Presidential Transition in Higher Education: Managing Leadership Change* (Baltimore, MD: The Johns Hopkins University Press, 2004).

2. Association of Governing Boards of Universities and Colleges, *Presidential Search Guidelines and Directory* (Washington, DC, 2005).

CHAPTER 12

Preparing for the Search

The next several chapters provide a detailed examination of the executive search process for selecting presidents and vice presidents. If the committee is working without a consultant, these chapters describe all the responsibilities that need to be carried out, enabling the search chair and staff supporting the search to plan for them. The underlying premise is that you can do almost everything the search consultant would do if you understand what that is and have the time to devote to it and the resources to support it. If the search committee is working with a consultant, these chapters will prepare the chair and others for the search by familiarizing them with significant details and options.

STEP 1: ORIENTING THE SEARCH COMMITTEE AND THE STAFF MEMBERS WHO ARE SUPPORTING THE SEARCH

The First Committee Meeting

The first meeting of the search committee is an important occasion. If you are working without a consultant, the chair should set an agenda that addresses the items described here. If you have a consultant, he or she will typically expect to meet with the search committee at the start of the search for a couple of hours (as well as meeting with many others on campus).

- *What are you looking for in your next president or vice president?* What is essential, and what is nice but optional? Which responsibilities can be delegated, and which must be the responsibility of the president himself or herself? This is the most important topic and one that all committees should discuss, whether or not they have consulting support. Some committees organize campus forums to involve others in the conversation about qualifications and characteristics of the new president.

- *What is the range of opinion among constituencies regarding what they are looking for?* The institution with seriously divergent expectations for the president will have a difficult search process. It is essential to discuss these topics and to consider how the discrepancies can be addressed. Discrepant perspectives that have not been resolved or at least addressed will make the position less attractive to candidates and will make it more difficult to reach agreement on whom to appoint.

- *Is there clarity about major issues of strategic direction?* Some institutions are facing major strategic decisions about overall enrollment size, or whether to build or expand graduate programs, or whether to establish a medical school. It is preferable to have made these major decisions as part of a strategic planning process before the search begins, so that candidates can be recruited who bring familiarity with the issues.

- *How likely are you to get what you are looking for?* Institutional ambition is a desirable and attractive characteristic, but institutional self-delusion can be a barrier to a successful search. Seek an impartial appraisal of the attractiveness of the position you are filling, perhaps by talking with the leaders of other institutions in your region or of your type. If you are working with a consultant, talk with him or her about whether the kind of candidate you are interested in is likely to be interested in you.

- *Can you provide an attractive compensation package?* Most committees do not get involved in the details of the compensation package (including salary and the potential for tenure and rank), leaving this to the board or the president. However, good candidates are often lost because the compensation package is not perceived to be adequate, so the committee should have a realistic understanding of how competitive the compensation package will be. There are two general views often found in the committee. One view is that administrative salaries are too high and should be kept more in line with faculty and staff salaries. The other view is that in order to attract the strongest candidates, the compensation package should be as substantial as possible. The latter view is sometimes accompanied by the speculation that "all boats rise on a rising tide," and if the president and vice president are well paid, that the salaries of others will gradually rise as well. Addressing this issue early in the search can reduce misunderstandings in the committee later on.

- *What is your recruiting strategy?* Develop a recruiting strategy, or ask your consultant to describe the strategy that he or she plans to use. If you are a third-tier institution in your *U.S. News and World Report* category, you or your consultant will probably be looking for candidates in tier three and tier two for your type of institution. If you are a denominational institution, you should contact other institutions of your denomination and perhaps of other denominations with which yours has some affinity. If you are considering abandoning your church relationship or allowing it to become less prominent over the next decade, or if on the contrary you want to maintain and even strengthen your church relationship, make sure you have a very clear understanding with the board before you begin recruiting, and shape your recruiting efforts accordingly.

- *Where will the position be advertised?* Do you plan to advertise the position and, if so, what venues will you use and what will be the nature of the advertisement? How many times will the ad appear? Do you have an advertising budget that must be respected? Work closely with your marketing department so that the ad is consistent with current marketing initiatives, and so that the current institutional logo is made available. If you are working with a consultant, decide who will place the ads. (See below for additional observations about advertising.)

- *What will the general timetable be?* Consider the urgency of your search. Is the current president leaving in three months, creating some pressure for an appointment promptly so that an interim appointment can be avoided? Or is the appointment of an interim president a desirable step, allowing time for an unhurried search and for the campus to get used to the idea that a beloved 25-year president has moved on? Think about issues of institutional momentum; campuses that are about to launch a strategic planning process may be eager to have a new president to shape and lead that process, not wanting to lose momentum.

- *What will the specific search schedule be?* Calendars fill up fast. It can be useful to set a meeting schedule for the full search at the first meeting. On the other hand, it may be difficult to predict when a strong pool will be assembled, so you may prefer to set the schedule as the search evolves. A sample search schedule is in Appendix F.

- *If you are working with a consultant, what role will he or she play?* For example, what information will the consultant provide for you about the candidates? Will the consultant deal with the candidates who applied for the position, or only with those who were recruited? Who will receive and respond to the candidate files that are submitted, and to the nominations? Will candidates be required to submit files electronically so that they can be placed on a password-protected Web site for committee review?

- *How will meetings be conducted?* If you are working without a search consultant, the committee chair will set meeting agendas, lead the meetings, and periodically inform the campus community of progress. If you have a consultant, the chair may want to rely fully on the consultant to carry out these tasks, or the chair may plan to do these things or to assign them to others, seeking only occasional input from the consultant. Often these allocations of responsibility emerge as the tasks come up, but if you prefer to clarify them in advance, this is the time to do it.

- *Procedural rules, including confidentiality and guidelines for communication with the press:* In most states, and in private institutions, confidentiality is a fundamental principle that must be discussed again and again to remind all participants of its importance, and to reinforce the message that there should be no conversations outside the committee during the search and forever after. Communication with the press is also an important issue. Often the student press is the most interested in the search and they may ask some of the most difficult questions. The typical rule is that only the search chair speaks for the search committee (see the sample code of ethics, Appendix E).

  Some states have what are known as "sunshine laws." These laws govern the openness of various government actions to public view. Some states require that their public colleges and universities conduct some or all of their searches publicly. In the most extreme case, the name of every individual mentioned to the search committee or the search consultant, even a name received only as a nomination without the candidate's knowledge or consent, must be made public. In other states, candidates are asked whether they wish their names to be kept confidential, and only the names of the five candidates recommended to the state system as finalists must be made public. The local media may choose to pursue the search committee aggressively, sending reporters to attend meetings or waiting outside the interview room for a candidate to appear. Or the media may choose to wait until the final stages of the search before seeking information about candidates. Once the finalists are named, reporters vary in how deeply they choose to dig into candidates' background; some go to the home campus of the finalists to interview colleagues and students. For committee members, the basic premise in all these situations is that only the committee chair should communicate on behalf of the committee.

- *Topics that are not permissible:* Most people know that there are several topics about which candidates cannot be asked, and that cannot be used as the basis for a committee decision. Age, race, ethnicity, marital status, family status, and sexual orientation are typically on this list. The state or city in which the institution is located may protect additional categories of individuals, and the institution may have additional protected categories as well. Often the director of human resources, diversity, or affirmative action is asked to meet with the committee to discuss these guidelines.

- *Diversity expectations:* Virtually all institutions emphasize the importance of attracting a diverse group of candidates. The committee should discuss how important this is, and the particular dimensions of diversity that may be most important—typically gender and ethnicity. If you are working without a consultant, be sure to build diversity recruiting into your recruiting strategy; you should of course expect a consultant to do this as well.

Working with Support Staff

The committee chair and the consultant should meet with the institutional staff members who are supporting the search. Most consulting firms provide some administrative support for the search, but the institution is normally asked to carry some of this responsibility as well. Most searches that use consultants expect the consultant's office to respond to candidates' questions and to receive and respond to nominations and applications. If your institution decides to receive these materials, your administrative support staff will have to establish a system for logging in, responding to, and tracking candidate files; additional details about how to do this are provided below. If you are working with a consultant, he or she can provide advice about how best to do this and how to coordinate the work of the campus and the consulting firm.

Setting Up a Public Web Page

The staff members supporting the search should establish an easily accessible page on the institution's Web site for all those with an interest in the search, including candidates and members of the institutional community and the external community. The content of that page can include a list of committee members; contact information for the person designated to receive nominations, input, or questions (normally the search committee chair and/or the consultant); information about the position (described below); and a general schedule for the search. Public institutions may be obliged to provide a detailed schedule, but providing a general schedule is preferable, allowing some flexibility for the committee to modify the schedule if needed. Public institutions are also sometimes obliged to post minutes of their meetings. In most states, those minutes include a record of the search process but do not include discussions of individual candidates

Anticipating the Scheduling of Interviews

The most substantial and even daunting task for the institution's support staff is to manage the campus interviews; even if you are working with a consultant, this task must be managed by a staff member on campus. The task is daunting because so many participants are involved and so many are eager to participate in the campus interviews. Coordinating calendars, respecting scheduling preferences, publicizing events, and finding meeting rooms are challenging assignments. The committee will establish a general interview schedule and provide a list of participants and invitees, and the staff implements that schedule. As soon as the committee can state with confidence the time period when these interviews will occur, those dates should be announced. This substantially increases the chances that the staff will be able to find time on the calendars of the key participants in the search.

STEP 2: ENGAGING THE CAMPUS COMMUNITY

Because the bulk of the committee's work will be carried out in confidence, it is important to make the search inclusive by allowing the campus to participate actively at the start of the search, during the planning stage. The committee can hold open forums for the full campus or for each constituency, and can meet with groups and individuals to gather their input. Forums can be supplemented by Web-based feedback mechanisms and articles in the campus newspaper. The open forums provide the basis for developing an in-depth understanding of the position. These conversations are important for many reasons. For the search committee, they reveal the extent of consensus or divergence in campus opinion. These conversations can be especially revealing for board members whose prior knowledge has been filtered through the outgoing president. For the consultant, the open forums also provide a sense of the campus culture and whether, for example, it is marked by civility and mutual respect, or by demoralization or acrimony. They give the consultant an opportunity to make an appraisal of the senior team that can later be discussed with key board members and in some cases with candidates. The more the consultant knows about the institution, the better able he or she is to represent it to candidates. For example, the consultant might assure candidates that the senior team is highly skilled and smoothly functioning, or might let them know that, if appointed, they should expect to have to do some team-building and perhaps hiring.

The observations that consultants share with candidates often carry greater weight than the same comments shared by board members or by employees of the institution. This is because the consultant is seen as a relatively impartial outsider with considerable professional knowledge of the field and of other institutions, and therefore seems worth listening to. For all these reasons, it is important that the consultant has an understanding that is as accurate as possible. If you are working without a consultant, you will want to assign the task of recruiting candidates to committee members who are similarly able to convey both enthusiasm and candor and to build trust with candidates.

The broad campus meetings are also valuable because they serve the campus and support the search process. These discussions are an opportunity for the campus to gain an understanding of the search process, to develop confidence in the committee, and, if there is a consultant, to gain confidence in the consultant's expertise and grasp of the particular situation. Key groups and individuals who have opportunities to talk with the consultant at the start of the search normally feel as a result that they have been listened to and that their opinion counts. Including individuals such as major donors in the process can be a cultivating tool for the next gift. Scheduling a meeting with the committee for members of the external community can be a step toward enhanced town-gown relations.

STEP 3: PREPARING RECRUITING MATERIALS
The Position Specification

Out of all these conversations and a review of key institutional documents, a position specification, or "spec," is typically developed. This document serves as a primary recruiting piece for your search. It is drafted either by the consultant or by a committee member, but in all cases it is ultimately approved by the search committee. Specs vary from a couple of pages to a dozen or more, and they can be simple or extremely elaborate full-color documents with photographs. The extent of polish is part of the image that you want to convey to prospective candidates. While the spec should look good in print form, many candidates will receive it by e-mail and will review it on their computer screens. The advantage of electronic documents is obviously that they can be distributed much more rapidly and can be posted on Web sites (typically the Web sites of both the consulting firm and the institution) so that anyone can see it at any time without relying on an intermediary, and without exposing his or her interest in the position. In addition, the electronic spec can include hyperlinks to other Web sites (e.g., the institution's strategic plan, or the Chamber of Commerce Web site for the region where the institution is located).

Looking beyond appearances, the content of the spec is a critical element in the recruiting process. These documents are intended to accomplish several goals. Most obviously, they attract candidates by describing the positive features of the position, the institution, and the location. They provide, in a single integrated document, information that would otherwise have to be ferreted out from many different documents and Web sites.

There are also more substantive issues surrounding the content of the spec. The exercise of writing this document can tease out issues that might otherwise be glossed over (e.g., whether a Ph.D. is required for this position, or an Ed.D. or a J.D.). It can clarify priorities. (For instance, will the vice president for advancement be expected to manage a portfolio of major donors, or will he or she spend most of his or her time supervising other development professionals and staffing the president's work with donors?)

Some committee members want to convey only the most positive and compelling aspects of the position, seeing the document as a marketing "puff piece." In my view, the spec should establish candor in the committee's relationship with the candidate. This may entail revealing some of the less favorable aspects of institutional life, which may concern committee members who think the spec should be a marketing piece that emphasizes only the positives, saving the negatives for private conversations at a later stage in the search. Taking a purely positive approach has limitations. Identifying the challenges associated with the position can be attractive to candidates. Most potential presidents and vice presidents not only are aware that their jobs entail dealing with challenges—they embrace this aspect of the role and are eager to be problem solvers. But in addition, reserving the concerns for a later stage in the process does not convey the candor that can form the basis of a healthy long-term relationship with candidates. A middle ground may be to allude to challenges without providing details at early stages; e.g., mention budgetary challenges, but hold back the full details of a deficit and the full audited financial statement until candidates reach a later stage in the search and the pool has been narrowed. This approach also has the advantage of restricting access to confidential or controversial information. Another approach is to mention an institutional problem while showing that steps are being taken to solve it, or to show that the problem is not so bad when seen in the context of other similar institutions (for example, a retention rate that seems low may actually be good when compared to the rates at institutions that admit students with similar academic profiles).

Because the spec will be widely available, including posting on the institution's Web site, it may have many audiences other than candidates. It may be seen by students and parents, by prospective students, by donors, by reporters, by outside critics, and so on. If the spec mentions concern about the low academic standards for admission, current students may feel denigrated. If the spec mentions unusually high endowment spending rates, donors may be worried about the eroding value of their gifts. These are serious concerns, but in my experience the concerns are often exaggerated. Few people outside the intended audience seem to take much interest in reading the recruiting documents. But having said this, the spec is a very public document and the committee needs to be able to stand behind its content, its accuracy, and its appropriateness. Sometimes features of an institution that are regularly discussed and clearly recognized by everyone in the institution (e.g., admission of students with limited academic potential) are alarming to committee members when seen in written and public form. The committee will need to agree on how to frame its description of the institution and the position in ways that are both attractive and honest, and with which the committee can be comfortable.

Typically, a position specification contains three kinds of information:

- A *position description and analysis,* including, for example, the responsibilities of the vice president for enrollment management; the place of the position in the organizational structure—to whom it reports, what positions are its peers, and what positions or offices report to it; what particular issues the appointee will be asked to address and what goals are to be accomplished in the long term and the short term;

- An *institutional description,* including, for example, history; mission, vision, and strategic plan; institutional culture and values; academic programs, both current and anticipated; a profile of the student body; financial resources available for accomplishing institutional goals and the goals of the particular position; and fund-raising status and capacity, including current and anticipated capital campaigns;

- *Application information,* including the information that candidates are expected to provide when they apply, the target date for candidate responses, contact information for the consultant and/or the search committee, salary range or a characterization of the range (e.g., "salary is highly competitive," or "salary is competitive for this type of institution").

Approval and Circulation
of the Position Specification

The approval of this document by the search committee is essential. A presidential search spec should reflect the intentions of the governing board, although the board may delegate its approval authority to the executive committee or to the board members on the search committee. The spec for a vice presidential search should be approved by the president. It is easy to see that a document of this complexity could be the subject of a year of deliberation! But the search must get started. I suggest that the committee take responsibility for approving the document and then provide it to key audiences for their information before beginning extensive circulation or posting on the Web site. The committee might, for example, send the completed spec to the full board, to the cabinet, to the governing bodies of the faculty, staff, and students, or to the full population of the campus. In doing so, it is essential to be very clear about whether comments and revisions are invited, and to be prepared to deal with the likely consequences of inviting those comments.

Most institutions create a Web page for presidential and vice presidential searches, placing an announcement on the institution's home page that allows the reader to go directly to the search page. You can visit the Web sites of other institutions that have recently had executive searches, or your consultant may have suggestions as to what to include. Following are some possibilities:

- *The position specification* is the central element of the search Web site.
- *Press releases* that accompanied the announcement of the vacancy.
- *A list of search committee members.* Normally this list omits contact information for all except the chair and/or the consultant.
- *Periodic updates on the progress of the search,* e.g., "The search committee is pleased to report that, following the careful review of a very strong pool of candidates, we have selected a small group of candidates for preliminary interviews. While we are maintaining complete confidentiality about our candidates, we will be updating this site periodically as the search proceeds to keep you informed of our progress."
- *A general statement of the search timetable.* For example, you might say, "the search committee will be recruiting and screening candidates throughout the fall semester and anticipates bringing three or four candidates to campus for interviews early in the spring semester."

In public institutions, committees sometimes post a detailed search schedule. This may be helpful to candidates, providing them with a clear sense of the process being followed, but it is hazardous for the committee; unforeseen events can lead to changes in the schedule, and changes will always raise questions and invite interpretation even when they were caused by something as innocent as a blizzard or a schedule conflict. If possible, post only a general schedule (e.g., "recruiting will occur during October and November, and candidates will be brought to campus for extensive interviews in January"). Search committees in public institutions also sometimes post the minutes of their meetings, but typically these reflect only the open portions of the meeting, omitting the confidential candidate information discussed in closed session.

Recruiting Packets

As your candidate pool develops, a small group of especially promising candidates is likely to emerge. The committee or the consultant, to cultivate the interest of these promising candidates, will want to provide them with substantial information about the position and the institution. A staff member supporting the search should assemble packets of information that can be sent to these candidates. The items in these packets will depend on the nature of the position; a packet for a presidential search will include campaign materials and strategic plans; materials for the provost search will include detailed materials about academic programs; and the CFO search packet will emphasize financial information. But there is a core of items that most search packets will normally include:

- Catalogs and view-books
- Strategic plan
- Fact book
- Planning documents
- Accreditation self-study and response (if they are recent)
- Budget and audited financial statement
- Organization chart
- Campaign materials and reports
- Sample copies of student newspapers and internal newsletters and alumni publications
- Materials describing the local community

Since these packets are sent only to the most promising candidates, some relatively confidential information may be included, although the most confidential items will likely be saved for finalists (for example, general financial information might be shared with all promising candidates, but the audited financial statement might be sent only to finalists. The need for clearer personnel policies might be shared with the promising candidates, but the complete lack of position descriptions, evaluations, and accountability might be discussed only with the finalists). The level of openness is a matter of campus culture, but building a relationship with candidates of mutual respect and honesty requires both the committee and the candidate to be candid. Information about institutional financial health is essential for presidential candidates, but many say that it was not provided during the search. As noted above, 20 percent of presidents said that they did not receive full financial information about the institution during the search. That figure rises to over 25 percent among presidents of private institutions.[1] Committees should strive to provide finalists with all necessary information.

NOTES

1. Melanie Corrigan, *The American College President* (Washington, DC: American Council on Education, 2002), 45.

CHAPTER 13

Recruiting Candidates

STEP 4: ADVERTISING

Virtually all senior searches in higher education are advertised. The best candidates rarely enter the search in response to ads, but there is still great value in advertising. Advertising is a visibility opportunity for the institution, allowing institutions that are not well known to showcase their existence and their distinctive character, and allowing better-known institutions to highlight their accomplishments and aspirations. For example, a locally based institution might attract attention nationally by stating "_____ University, a thriving and entrepreneurial institution located in the rapidly growing suburbs of the city of _____, seeks a president able to build bridges to the affluent community surrounding our institution while serving an underserved, ethnically diverse student body." A national university might draw attention to its aspirations by selecting key passages from the president's address to the faculty: "It is now incumbent on us to implement a vision for the future that continues to move our University ever higher in the ranks of the world's preeminent universities...to shape our institution into a truly global university which is deeply rooted in this community, which is passionately committed to advancing human civilization, and which provides for our students an education that is second to none."[1]

While some of your strongest prospective candidates may be well aware of the vacancy you are seeking to fill, others may not. In fact, some may never have heard of your institution. An additional value of advertising is that it alerts potential candidates to the opportunity; they may or may not respond directly to the ad, but they might begin to think about it. When the search chair or the consultant contacts them to explore their interest in the position, candidates sometimes say, "I saw that ad and have been thinking about it, but I have some questions." Some candidates even say, "I saw that ad and I was wondering when you would call me." The ad has great value in triggering nominators to consider colleagues ready to make a move and may lead them to submit their candidate suggestions. If you have a consultant, he or she will be doing extensive outreach, but the ad prepares the field for those more targeted efforts.

Some institutions prefer to place the ads themselves, while others ask the search consultant to handle this step. In either case, someone should carefully proofread the text and should be responsible for reading the ad when it appears in all venues in print and online. If there are errors, they should be corrected and, depending on the source of the error, the bill might be adjusted.

Enhancing Diversity

Most institutions are striving to diversify the group of candidates they can consider, and advertising provides a way of insuring that all potential candidates are aware of the position. The recruiting strategy developed by the committee or the consultant will be designed to attract a diverse pool, and advertising is part of this strategy. In addition to the publications that serve a broad audience (such as the *Chronicle of Higher Education*), there are some focused on particular populations (e.g., women, members of racial and ethnic minorities). Searches striving to attract these populations may want to consider advertising in these venues. *Diverse Issues in Higher Education* focuses on the African-American community and other diverse groups in higher education. *Hispanic Outlook, Women in Education,* and the gender-based or ethnicity-focused groups within some professional associations can provide advertising venues. These venues have particular symbolic value in signaling an interest in the communities served by the publication.

The Style and Content of Advertisements

As you review the ads in publications that focus on higher education, you will see a variety of approaches. Some ads simply say in essence, "We have a vacancy and here is how to contact us." Most ads are somewhat more substantial but omit a great deal of detail, referring readers to a Web site that can provide additional information. And at the other extreme, some ads are extremely detailed, providing considerable specific information about the institution and the position. Since most publications charge by the inch, this is partly a matter of budget. In some institutions, it is a quasi-legal matter; the institution's human resources policy may require that the advertisement include extensive details, while the policy at other institutions may allow those details to be provided elsewhere.

The text of the advertisement should be fully consistent with the position specification. Search committees are often eager to place the ad and launch the search, but it is unwise to place the ad before the position specification is at least in final draft, and before the consultant is selected, if you are using a consultant. Changes in the spec may cause you to wish you could change the ad, but you discover it is too late. You will also want to note in the ad that the position specification is available on your Web site; if it is not yet completed, prospective candidates may look for it in vain, and the committee will not look fully in command of the search process.

Online Advertising

Online position listings also provide a vehicle for letting potential candidates and nominators know about your search. They are of two types. There are fairly generic Web sites that attract a very broad audience, and often these sites make it very simple for a candidate to respond and send you an application. Committees may be attracted to the broad exposure, but these sites rarely attract candidates well suited to senior positions in higher education. The second type of online position listing is targeted to a particular audience; these listings are more likely to bring your position to the attention of the people in whom you are most interested. For example, there are online listings for financial officers, for institutions of specific religious affiliations, and so on. These are typically more productive and should be explored. The cost of online position listings is lower than the cost of print advertising, often by a factor of 10.

STEP 5: RECEIVING AND RESPONDING
TO APPLICATIONS

As soon as your ad appears, you will begin to receive applications. Some search committees prefer to receive applications directly, even though they may be working with a consultant. Moreover, some consultants specify that they will receive only the materials of the candidates they are recruiting, preferring that candidates who are responding to the ad be directed to send their materials to the search committee. This is a matter that you should clarify when selecting your consultant. I will discuss the elements of candidate file management and then the allocation of responsibility between the committee and the consultant, if one is used.

- *Establishing a log of all candidate activity:* Before the first nomination or application is received, a system should be established that logs in every individual who is part of the search process. Every candidate and nominee should be listed, and provision should be made to show their current status and their changing status as the search proceeds. The log should note every item of correspondence with the candidate or critical decision made about the candidate (e.g., application acknowledged, invitation to interview extended, application withdrawn, application rejected by the committee).

- *Responding to nominations:* The nominator should be acknowledged and the nominee should be notified and invited to apply. If there is reason to think the nominee could be a promising candidate, the log should flag the nominee for additional pursuit.

- *Responding to applications:* All applications should be acknowledged. If this is not done quickly, you will find many candidates e-mailing or phoning to ask whether the materials have been received. To avoid this extra workload, and to show from the start that this search is being handled with professionalism and respect for candidates, the acknowledgement should be very prompt (ideally within a day or two).

- *Requesting missing information:* Occasionally, applications will have missing elements. A candidate might not include the requested list of references, or the curriculum vitae might arrive without a cover letter. The committee should decide how to handle this situation; if there is a consultant, his or her advice should be sought. Some might consider the absence of part of the normal application packet to be a disqualifier. Others might be willing to consider whatever is submitted, without concern for missing items, as long as the core information is provided. And others might wish to notify candidates of missing items and request that they be provided. My recommendation is that the information submitted should be screened; if this appears to be a strong candidate, the missing items should be requested, but if it appears to be a weak candidate, for whom additional items are unlikely to strengthen the case, those items should not be requested. Some committees will wish to treat candidates uniformly; although this serves the goal of equity, and the institution's legal counsel may encourage this approach, it also burdens weak candidates with requests for information that are not, in the end, likely to improve their standing.

- *Screening:* Some searches have a set of minimum criteria and, if they are not met, candidates will not be reviewed further. In these cases, a basic review of all applicants might lead to some being notified that they are no longer under consideration. If the position requires a doctoral degree, for example, applicants without that degree might be thanked and told that, because of this requirement, their candidacy can not be considered further.

- *Tracking changed status:* As described above, the candidate log should reflect every element of correspondence and every change of status. The log has to be maintained and updated, noting the content of phone calls with the committee chair, the date when a packet of material was sent, and the nominee's decision to apply or to decline.

- *Notifying candidates of changed status:* When the search committee changes a candidate's status, he or she should be notified appropriately. For example, if the candidate is not to be invited to a preliminary interview, or to a second-round interview, he or she should be notified promptly. This is another crucial element of the professionalism and respect for candidates shown by your search. Failure to update candidates promptly and to keep them informed respectfully is one of the things that candidates complain about most often. While you might consider that some of these complaints are not justified (e.g., the candidate who says, "When my application was rejected and I was not invited for an interview, someone should have phoned me to tell me personally and provide feedback"), the way candidates are treated will be part of the reputation of the search, the institution, and of course the consultant.

Having laid out the key elements of file management, I want to return to the question of assigning responsibility for these tasks.

Coordination between Committee and Consultant

If the consultant receives all materials from all candidates, the role of the search chair is a great deal simpler. The consultant and his or her colleagues carry out all the tasks described above, within the guidelines agreed to with the committee. The chair's involvement can be focused on special cases, such as answering particularly complex questions from candidates that exceed the consultant's familiarity with the institution. The consultant may also ask the chair to help recruit very promising but reluctant presidential candidates who are not sure, for example, whether the board is willing and able to make contributions that are adequate to support institutional aspirations, or vice presidential candidates who want to test the chemistry with the president or to get a clearer sense of the president's vision.

Consultants who receive all candidate materials will have some agreement with the search committee as to which files will be forwarded for committee review, and how and when they will be forwarded. The consultant may offer to screen the candidate pool and send forward only the five or 10 most outstanding candidates. The committee might (or might not) receive a list of all applicants, but would not receive their files. In this mode, the consultant vastly streamlines the committee's work, but the committee gives up control over a portion of the selection process.

The consultant may offer to send the committee all candidate files that are received, whether the candidates applied in response to an ad or were recruited actively by the consultant. Those files might or might not be evaluated or screened by the consultant. In this mode, the committee's work is substantial —screening and evaluating all the candidate files—but the committee retains full control over the critical matter of which candidates are selected for further attention.

A mixed approach is for the consultant to screen and evaluate all the candidate files, while also providing all the files for committee review. Committee members are free to read all files and compare their evaluations to the consultant's evaluations, but those who wish to read only the files recommended by the consultant can focus their attention on the recommended files. This approach balances the work that committee members have to do and their control over candidate selection.

Once the questions above are resolved, a mechanism should be established for transfer of files from the consultant's office to the committee. Increasingly this is done electronically; candidates submit their materials using e-mail, and the consultant transmits them electronically to the committee chair or administrative staff. E-mail is vastly simpler and faster than transmitting paper files.

Some search committees prefer to receive all materials directly from candidates. Some committee members feel that this signals a greater level of engagement of the committee in the process, and a more academic character to the search. This view is not a common one, and most chairs are eager to shift the considerable burdens described above to the consulting firm. Few institutions are able to provide sufficient administrative support staff to handle these tasks smoothly, and recognize that the search firm is organized to handle them routinely. For those searches that do choose to receive all files, the steps described above are simply reversed—that is, instead of the consultant sending files to the campus, the campus sends them to the consultant so that he or she can follow up as needed by contacting nominees, cultivating the strongest candidates, and so on.

In some searches, there is an agreement that the consultant will receive only the materials of recruited candidates, while the committee receives the materials of applicants responding to the advertisement. The committee screens the applicant files and, if they identify any that seem promising and worthy of further cultivation, those files can be passed to the consultant for follow-up.

Setting Up a Secure Web Page

When it is time for committee members to review candidate files, most committees post the electronic candidate files on a password-protected area of their Web site or on a page of their courseware. The search is treated as though it was a course and only "students" in the course—i.e., committee members—are given access to the site. Even those who are not frequent Web users are usually able to learn quickly to access the site, and of course this approach has the value of making files accessible anywhere the reader is able to get on line.

The more difficult question is whether committee members are able to read files on their screens, or need to print out every file. My suggestion for those uncomfortable with on-screen review is that they make an initial review of the file on the screen. Files of promising candidates can be printed out for further scrutiny, with the ability to make marginal notes and to bring the files and notes to committee meetings.

Some committees worry about the security of electronic files, and it may be true that the risk of unintentional or intentional massive dissemination of candidate files by e-mail is greater with electronic files than the risk of dissemination of paper files. But in my experience the risk can be reduced by regular reminders about security. The trade-off is a substantially enhanced process for the committee.

STEP 6: RECEIVING NOMINATIONS AND FOLLOWING UP ON THEM

As soon as the ad appears, you will also begin to receive nominations. A staff member should be assigned to follow up on all nominations, including the following steps:

- Send a letter or e-mail to thank the nominator.

- Notify the nominee and invite him or her to apply for the position. Some nominators do not wish to be identified to their nominees (e.g., if a vice president nominates a direct report, the implication—accurately or not—might be that a departure is being encouraged). If nominees ask who nominated them, provide that information only if the nominator has said you may do so.

- Log in all nominations and have a plan for matching nominations with the application that may later arrive from the nominee.

- One or more committee members should review nominations and, if the nominee seems especially promising but does not respond to the nomination, should follow up with the nominees and encourage them to become candidates.

Nominations are one of the most potentially valuable items in a search. A nomination, particularly from someone whose opinion is especially respected, calls for careful attention by the committee chair or the consultant. If the nominee is already known to and highly regarded by the chair or the consultant, the nomination can be a reinforcement of the committee's or consultant's interest, or a reminder that this is someone to pursue. Candidates are often flattered to be nominated and pleased to engage in a conversation about the position, and they may even respond quickly to a notice that they have been nominated by sending an application, not needing any further convincing.

Conversations with Nominees

Even when a strong candidate responds promptly to a nomination by submitting application materials, additional contact and cultivation may be appropriate. The chair or consultant may want to do some screening to determine the fit of this person with this position, may want to prepare a report for the committee about the candidate and the reason for his or her interest, or may have some particular questions to ask (such as, "We are very interested in you because you have such a fine reputation, but I notice that you have only been at your current institution for two years. Can you tell me more about why you would want to make a move so soon?").

Candidates Who Decline Nominations

Some candidates decline a nomination and really do not wish to pursue this particular search, no matter how persuasive the consultant or the search chair may be. But sometimes a call can persuade them to change their minds and at least take a preliminary look at this search. The call to a candidate who has declined can also be a valuable opportunity to discuss the nomination of others; someone who would have been a good candidate if he or she had been interested is likely to be able to suggest other good candidates.

Nominees decline nominations for many reasons, some totally unrelated to the attractiveness of the opportunity. But the consultant and the committee should keep an eye out for patterns in the explanations for declining; learning more about these explanations is another reason why it might be useful to phone a candidate who declined a nomination. For example, if promising nominees decline to apply because they have heard that there is an inside candidate who has a lock on the position, and candidates cannot be persuaded that this is truly an open search, the committee should be aware of this, because their pool is like to be weaker or smaller as a result. But if there is no inside candidate, or no one with an inside track to the position, the conversation can seek to overcome this reservation and perhaps persuade the nominee to apply. If promising nominees decline to apply because they have heard that there are financial problems at the institution, the committee may need to assemble information that overcomes that objection, or may want to talk with the board about the heightened expectations that a new president is likely to have for board members' philanthropic contributions. In some cases, the chair might ask the chief financial officer to call this potential candidate to address his or her concerns. Sometimes the reasons that promising candidates decline to apply go to the heart of an institution's identity and are not easily addressed. Examples include a single-sex institution whose community is divided about coeducation, or an ambitious institution that is divided as to whether the new president should be primarily an academic leader or a fundraiser. Although these are not insurmountable issues, and some potential candidates will see them as exciting challenges, they may call for some institutional soul-searching and extensive communication on critical topics with the strongest candidates.

Dealing with Weak Nominees

While many nominees are outstanding potential candidates, there are some nominees who are quite weak. Nominators sometimes are sympathetic to a colleague who has run into trouble, has to leave his or her position, and is looking for a new job as quickly as possible. Some nominators are simply accommodating a request from a friend or colleague who asked if they could provide a nomination. Some nominators misunderstand the nature of the institution and the position; for example, someone at a large, complex, and prominent institution may nominate a junior colleague to be chief academic officer at a smaller regional institution, thinking that their lack of experience will not be a problem in such a simple institution. While some nominations offer highly promising candidates, others do not. A call to the nominator may clarify the reason for his or her support of this candidate and the strength of the endorsement. I encourage notifying all nominees that they have been nominated and inviting them to apply. Once the chair or consultant has the opportunity to review the nominees' credentials, they will be able to sort the weak from the strong prospects and can follow up accordingly.

STEP 7: ACTIVE RECRUITING

With systems in place for receiving and responding to applications and nominations, you are ready to enter the heart of the search process—active recruiting. It is typically the reason why institutions hire search consultants and, although consultants do much more than recruit, recruiting is essential to serving clients successfully.

Formulating a Recruiting Plan

If you are seeking to model your search on a search conducted by a consultant, you should have an active recruiting plan. The plan should be driven by a sound understanding of the institution and its needs.

Begin by mapping out the *kind of institution* from which you think candidates are likely to come; these are typically peers of your institution, or institutions to which you aspire to be a peer. For example, a search at an AAU institution will likely focus on other AAU institutions or strong research institutions that are similar to AAU members. A comprehensive regional public institution might focus on members of the American Association of State Colleges and Universities (AASCU). This does not mean that candidates from elsewhere will be rejected—it simply means that you are focusing on the most likely and/or the ideal sources of candidates for your intensive recruiting efforts.

In addition to considering the associations to which institutions belong, consider focusing on institutions that are similarly structured and funded, with key common features like faculty collective bargaining agreements. These can also provide a set of peers (e.g., the campuses of California State University, the regional four-year campuses of the State University of New York, the regional state colleges and universities in New Jersey and Wisconsin). The *U.S. News and World Report* rankings can be a useful starting point; you might focus on the tier in which your institution is listed, plus one tier above and one tier below. Your institution may have developed a list of peer and aspiration institutions for use in benchmarking.

The exercise of selecting the target institutions can sometimes become controversial; to avoid the controversy, remember that, within reasonable limits, you should be open to creating a longer list that includes all the target institutions that are suggested, rather than a shorter list that rules many out. The controversy, if it occurs, usually grows out of a concern that the list determines where candidates will ultimately come from; reassure committee members that the list simply serves as a starting point for recruiting.

Focus next on the *kind of position* from which you think the candidates are likely to come. Presidential candidates are likely to be vice presidents or deans, or possibly presidents at smaller or less prominent institutions. Vice presidential candidates are likely to be associate vice presidents, deans, or directors, or possibly vice presidents with a narrower portfolio, or at smaller or less prominent institutions. Searches at public institutions would normally focus on recruiting from other publics, and privates from privates, but there are many cases in which crossover between public and private is very possible. For example, a private institution that emphasizes access and community engagement might find strong candidates in public institutions with similar missions. A top-tier public research university might find strong prospects in top-tier private research universities. The public-private distinction may be of greater significance for highly selective private liberal arts colleges, or for public institutions that are in systems, where a candidate's familiarity with this institutional type may be viewed as especially important.

Consider how *regional or national* your search should be. If your area of the country has very high housing costs, you may want to focus on candidates who already live in your region, or who live in other areas of high housing costs. If your institution is in the snowbelt, you may have less success recruiting in the South and might get a better return on your investment of time and effort if you recruit in regions of similar climate. Having said this, there may be some eager candidates who are happy to move from a mild to a cold climate because they enjoy skiing or because they have relatives in your area; finding these candidates will be more difficult, but sometimes they are uncovered through a series of calls in which you highlight the appeal of the area to certain kinds of people. In a search in Alaska, for example, you might seek candidates who are hunters or pilots or environmentalists and would find the location an attractive place to pursue these personal interests.

If a *diverse candidate pool* is important, as it virtually always is, there should be a strategy to recruit diverse candidates. There are several basic approaches. Special-interest publications can be used in advertising, as described above. The leaders of organizations focused on particular groups can sometimes suggest individuals who would be appropriate candidates for the particular search (for example, the offices within the American Council on Education). Women and people of color who hold positions elsewhere that are similar to the position you are filling will often be especially eager and able to suggest the names of other women and people of color who could be good candidates in your search. Call upon others in your institution, whether or not they are on the search committee, if they can help you to identify and recruit women and people of color to the candidate pool.

Some search committees are eager to see some *nontraditional candidates*—that is, candidates whose primary background is not in higher education but who have strong experience in other nonprofit organizations (e.g., health care, human services, government, the arts), or in the corporate world (law firms, consulting firms, financial services). This kind of candidate is more likely to be sought by trustees than by those internal to the institution. Trustees often think that a candidate from outside the academy will be more market-driven, customer service–oriented, and decisive, or that they will see the college or university as a business to be managed aggressively or entrepreneurially, and that these leaders from outside higher education will not tolerate the leisurely pace of faculty governance. The *American College President* report found that, of sitting presidents responding to a 2001 survey, 80 percent moved to the presidency from another presidency or a senior executive position in higher education, but almost 20 percent came from outside higher education (private business, government, religious roles outside higher education, K-12 administration and, the largest category in this nontraditional group, "other").[2] In my experience, search committees often ask to see nontraditional candidates but, when the search concludes, they are not so likely to recommend them, and boards are not so likely to appoint them.

Unfortunately, I know of no data that allow comparison of the leadership styles and institutional strategies of traditional candidates with strictly academic backgrounds, and the styles and strategies of nontraditional candidates who come from other sectors. We do not know whether the assumptions about entrepreneurial approaches and brisker decision making are accurate descriptions. We also do not know if traditional and nontraditional candidates are equally likely to be successful presidents or vice presidents in higher education.

Implementing the Recruiting Plan

The institutions, positions, and locations that are likely to yield candidates are now your targets. Typically consultants will cast a wide net and send e-mail messages or letters to this list, and the search committee should do so as well. Look up names on Web sites or in a higher education directory. Your message should be short and compelling.

If you do not get a response to your e-mail, you should phone to follow up, especially calling those prospects who seem most attractive. If committee members know some of the people listed in your recruiting plan, they should make those calls. Many of your calls may be "cold calls" to people you do not know, but who hold the right title. Encourage the person you are calling to consider the position, send them the materials you have prepared, and, if they decline and you cannot change their minds, ask them if they would like to suggest other potential candidates.

Compared to advertising and e-mailing, phoning prospective candidates is a far more effective recruiting strategy, but it is also more time consuming and therefore should be highly targeted. The consultant will have some trusted sources or potential candidates who go high on the call list, and the search chair and committee members will have some of these relationships too. As part of an aggressive recruiting strategy, you should expect to call relentlessly, working through your list of possible candidates, following up on candidate suggestions, leaving messages and calling repeatedly those people who have the greatest potential to add to the search. Most consulting firms maintain databases that assist them in this demanding phase of the search process, and the staff supporting your search should construct a similar database to keep track of your recruiting efforts.

During the recruiting period (normally six to eight weeks), the many potential and actual candidates will all be moving at different speeds, will have different concerns, and will need different kinds of responses. Some candidates will be unreachable until the very last minute and they will need to be told either that the deadline is inviolable, or that the candidate response date is just a target and that they should send materials even if the deadline has passed. Some may be assured that if all they can send is a CV, without a reference list or a cover letter, that will be just fine; in other searches, all these items and more may be required. The simpler the application process, the more likely that your search will be able to attract a candidate who is on the fence or who is too overwhelmed by other demands to prepare a complete set of materials. If your search has flexibility in the application process and the timing of responses, you should take advantage of this. There may be strong candidates who cannot comply with rigid search guidelines and the flexibility of your search will allow you to capture their attention.

Cultivation of Promising but Reluctant Candidates

Either through nominations or other recruiting, you will identify some potential candidates who seem very promising but are not initially interested in this position. In working with the reluctant candidate, some committees follow a consistent set of steps, making no special arrangements to attract prospective candidates, and dropping them if they express no initial interest. But these reluctant candidates may be some of the best candidates, and some institutions will want to make substantial effort to attract them. Phone calls can be made by individuals such as the consultant, the committee chair, the board chair, or key institutional officers or leaders. There can be cultivational visits by the candidate to the campus, outside the normal interview process and schedule, or visits by institutional representatives to the candidate. Taking these out-of-the-ordinary steps may be alarming to those who believe that every candidate should be treated the same. But every candidate does not offer the same capacity to succeed in the position, and most consultants will recommend that, having identified those who appear to have a great capacity for success, you should pursue them aggressively.

Bringing a potential candidate to campus for a visit outside the framework of the normal search process can be a powerful opportunity to provide the kind of insider insights that engage the candidate, highlight the institution's strengths (including the dedicated individuals who will meet the candidate), have a candid discussion of the institution's challenges, and begin to build strong relationships. Similarly, the committee chair or board chair can travel to visit the candidate, describing the great appeal of the institution and its aspirations for greatness toward which the candidate can so capably lead them. Either of these approaches is extremely flattering, and most candidates know that not everyone is getting this treatment. I have even had some candidates worry about the unfairness of the special attention they are receiving, but I assure them that we are giving special attention to all the candidates who are as strong as they are. Obviously you are not going to give this kind of attention to a candidate about whom you have reservations, hoping to avoid the awkwardness of initially convincing this person to apply, and then ultimately dropping him or her from further consideration.

Recruiting Pre-Qualified Candidates

There are some searches in which targets are drawn with such precision that only a small number of prospects is identified, and they are the only ones contacted. This is the extreme form of active recruiting. Background checks are done informally to be sure that the five or six target candidates are really right for the position. (For example, calling trusted sources to say, "I know you have worked with John—do you think he is someone we should recruit? Can you tell us about what it is like to work with him, what he has accomplished, and what kind of reputation he has?") This is not a reference call—it is a "sourcing" call to "prequalify" the candidate. If all the responses to this kind of inquiry paint an attractive picture, the candidate can be called with a very aggressive message, such as "We have heard a lot about you and we're calling to say that we would like to invite you to come and meet with the board chair." Leaping over the sending of application materials, the airport interview in which the candidate competes with 10 or 12 other candidates, and the screening and reference checking, this search process moves very quickly, avoiding the protracted period of time that elapses during each phase of the search. It is also likely to involve fewer participants in the search process and thus reduces the risk of breached confidentiality. It can be alarming to a prospective candidate to be virtually offered a position before he or she has even considered the opportunity, and some may be uninterested or even offended. However, it is more likely to be highly flattering, and that in itself has a persuasive effect.

NOTES

1. Steven B. Sample, *Annual Address to the Faculty, 2005* (Los Angeles, CA: University of Southern California, 2005).

2. Melanie Corrigan, *The American College President* (Washington, DC: American Council on Education, 2002), 104.

CHAPTER 14

Evaluating Candidates and Selecting Finalists

STEP 8: SCREENING CANDIDATE FILES

Once you have assembled a pool of candidates, the committee must screen them. It is difficult to predict how large the pool will be. Candidate pools in 2006 are smaller than they were 10 years ago. I suspect this is because the expectations for presidencies and vice presidencies have been heightened and that, as a result, fewer are qualified and even fewer are interested. But perhaps this will change and pools will grow again in the future as professional development programs prepare a new generation of leaders. Apart from these long-term changes, the number of candidates depends on the position, the institution, the institutional history, the compensation package, the location, and the time of year when the search occurs. Avoid focusing on the total number of candidates and focus instead on quality.

Reviewing Candidate Files

Reading candidate files can be a daunting task. The CVs of those with academic backgrounds can easily run to 20–50 pages, and the cover letters often are 10 pages long; this is a very different style of presentation from what a trustee might find in a corporate search. Appendix G offers suggestions for reviewing candidate materials that may simplify the process. As committee members read the files, they should focus on the position description that enumerated the characteristics they were looking for. A rating sheet can be constructed that reminds committee members of these characteristics and provides space for notes and a rating on each element, as well as an overall rating for each candidate. I prefer a three-point scale that can be construed as "high/medium/low" or "strong/moderate/weak" or "keep/not sure/drop" or "A/B/C". Appendix H includes a sample rating sheet.

The Initial Screening to Remove Unqualified Candidates

The first step in the process of screening candidates is to screen out the remarkably large number of candidates who are unqualified for your position; this can be done by the full committee, a subcommittee, or the consultant. In most searches, one-half to two-thirds of the candidates fall into this category. At the most basic level, a search requiring a certain educational credential may find applicants who simply do not have it (e.g., the Ph.D., or a doctorate of some sort). A search that has specified the need for certain institutional experience may find applicants who lack that experience (e.g., candidates for chief academic officer who have not worked in higher education, candidates for president of a research university whose only experience has been in a two-year institution, or candidates for president of a church-related institution who have no affinity for the denomination in particular or religion in general). A search at an elite private institution striving for even greater stature and recognition may find candidates whose only experience has been at open-admission public institutions. While the candidates may be excellent leaders and fine people, they are simply unlikely to be perceived as a good fit by the search committee, the board, and the campus community. Screening out these candidates means that not all members of the search committee have to read all these files.

Screening the Potentially Qualified Candidates

Once the applications from the clearly unqualified candidates have been set aside, there will be a group of candidates about whom more substantive discussion needs to occur.

At this stage, a consultant is likely to have valuable advice. He or she may know many of your candidates through a range of professional associations, or may have met or interviewed them in preparation for your meeting, or in the course of working on other searches. The consultant will respect the confidentiality of candidates and will not reveal which other searches they may have entered, but will share with the committee his or her appraisal of the candidates, and information gathered from previous reference calls.

Consultants vary in how they approach the identification of the strongest candidates; committees working with consultants should have a sense of the range of alternative approaches. Some consultants present a "slate" of candidates, identifying five or 10 candidates whom they believe are the best prospects for this position. This saves the committee from the effort of sorting through a lot of files to find the winners. Consultants who take this approach can be expected to bring you substantial information about the candidates being presented, including reports on their own preliminary interviews with candidates, one or more reference reports, the results of a check of computerized databases and on-line newspaper reports, and the backstory of the candidate's career—e.g., "He ran into trouble when he was a dean, but the campus was a notoriously difficult one and the candidate has gone on to have great success since then."

Other consultants do not present a slate or recommend candidates, allowing the committee to select candidates to focus on. But even with this approach, you should expect the consultant to bring you critical elements of information to assist with your selection process. The consultant should have had a phone interview, a video interview, or a face-to-face interview with most if not all of the candidates in whom the committee is likely to have greatest interest.

Complementing the consultant's information, committee members sometimes also know some of the candidates personally or by reputation. If the knowledge is many years old or was received thirdhand or as a general rumor, the chair might suggest that it not be shared with the committee. But if it is reasonably current and reliable, and if it does not violate legal limits on topics that can be used as the basis for decision making, this is useful information to share with the committee. Other committee members may or may not take that knowledge as determinative in their own appraisal of the candidate, but all available and appropriate information should be discussed. Some committee members may be concerned that this information is not available for all candidates. For example, a great deal more information will be available about internal candidates than about candidates who have never worked at the institution. These are the kinds of variations that cannot be controlled in the search process; I recommend bringing as much information as possible to the committee, even though that means more is known about some candidates than about others.

Selecting Candidates for Preliminary Interviews

Once the clearly unqualified candidates have been put aside and the additional insights of the consultant and committee members have been brought to bear in a discussion of candidates, the committee will have to select the candidates to be moved forward to the next stage of the search, which is typically a preliminary interview with the search committee.

The committee's screening process should be defined in a way that is consistent with the institutional culture and the preferences of the chair and the committee members. Some committees take votes and make decisions strictly based on the numbers. Other committees take a much more fluid approach in which there is a sense of the group but not a formal vote. Most committees take an approach somewhere in the middle, in which an initial screening vote is followed by a discussion of candidates in whom there is some interest. Most search consultants have had extensive experience with these processes and can help the committee to reach a decision that has general support while maintaining the committee's sense of mutual respect and teamwork.

A good starting point is to gather and tabulate the ratings of each candidate given by each reader. This can be done before the committee meeting, or the meeting can begin with a quick gathering of ratings (e.g., "Candidate Alan Adams—how many rated him A? How many B? How many C?...Candidate Barbara Bloom—how many rated her A? How many B? How many C?). Once this process is completed and the ratings tallied on a flipchart, you will see very quickly which candidates can be dropped without further discussion because they received virtually uniform C ratings, and which candidates should be discussed further. I recommend careful discussion of all candidates who are of interest to at least a few committee members; sometimes discussion leads to new insights and reconsideration of the initial appraisal of a candidate's strength.

Sometimes there is a clear consensus on which candidates to interview and which to drop, but usually there are a few candidates about whom opinion is divided. I recommend pursuing more candidates at this stage rather than fewer, and taking a chance on candidates who may not initially appear to be the strongest. Often the candidates who appear strongest turn out, in an interview, to be unimpressive, while the candidates who appear to be less strong on paper may be extremely compelling in an interview. Only further information gathering (in reference calls and background checks and extended conversations) will lead to final selection. At this early stage, cast a wide net.

If There Are Too Many Good Candidates

Sometimes there are more attractive candidates than there is time to interview. If there is an abundance of good candidates, those not initially invited to interview can be treated as alternates. Sometimes an invited candidate is unavailable, and an alternate can be invited to fill the vacant slot in the interview schedule. Once the preliminary interviews are over, if the committee still wants to see more candidates, alternates can then be invited. You may want to tell the candidate about this alternate status, but more likely you will want to avoid offending the candidate and try to mask the fact that he or she has been held in abeyance until the first-choice candidates have been seen.

If There Are Too Few Good Candidates

On the other hand, there may be only two or three candidates of interest to the committee, whereas they would have hoped for more. People often say, "Well, it only takes one." At this early stage, though, it is better to have many more than one. If your committee has very few candidates at this stage, you have two choices. You can forge ahead with the candidates you have and hope for the best. Or, you can continue recruiting. The advantage of continued recruiting is that you may be able to bring additional strong prospects into the pool and, if the process moves quickly, your search might be able to conclude on schedule. The disadvantage of continued recruiting is that, if your existing candidates become aware of it, they may be perplexed and even resentful that their candidacy is not sufficiently attractive to the committee. You should also guard against the sense that, if only we keep looking, the ideal candidate will be discovered.

STEP 9: PRELIMINARY INTERVIEWS
The Value of Preliminary Interviews

After having studied a candidate's letter of application and curriculum vitae with care, most committee members feel they have a sense (and some are certain that they have a *very* clear sense) of what the candidates are like and what they would bring to the position. But the first face-to-face contact is often a revelation. There can be a remarkable gap between the appraisal of a candidate based on written materials and the appraisal based on a face-to-face interview. And of course, both the documents and the preliminary interview assessment can turn out to be at odds with references and with actual performance on the job.

Interview performance is difficult to predict. Some candidates interview better than expected, and others interview less well than expected. Often committees select a preferred group of candidates to be invited to a preliminary interview, but add one last person as an alternate, or simply because there is an open time slot or because the candidate is nearby, and are surprised to discover that this candidate is the strongest of all. Because of this possibility, committees should meet more candidates rather than fewer, going beyond the list of clear favorites.

You should always be mindful that what you see in candidates, especially in the small one- or two-hour slice of exposure that the preliminary interview provides, is interview behavior, not real-life behavior. Candidates are anxious, no matter how sophisticated or experienced they may be. The interview conversation may appear to a committee member to be conversational, but the committee has wide discretion, within legal limits, to ask questions, while the candidate is obliged by the norms of the interview process to reply. The discussion is controlled by the committee, even when it provides an opportunity for the candidate to ask questions. The time period is fixed, so topics cannot be explored as they normally might, with the unstructured give-and-take of ideas that would occur in a normal conversation. I am not suggesting that these features should be changed, but committee members should remember that they are selecting a senior officer, not just a good interviewer. If a candidate's qualifications are strong but the interview is not compelling, consider whether the candidate might be better on the job than in the interview, and thus may merit further attention. In the hundreds of interviews I have observed, it is troubling to see how often style trumps substance, and the candidate with substantial skill and experience is dropped from further consideration because someone on the committee says "we just didn't connect" or "he never made eye contact with me."

In spite of the difficulty of appraising normal behavior on the job based on an interview, preliminary interviews are a valuable screening device. Even if your consultant has already interviewed your leading candidates, the committee should also interview them before bringing them to a wider audience such as the full board or the full campus community.

Research suggests that judgments made in the first few seconds of an encounter (an interview, or a course, or a cocktail party) correlate highly with the judgments made at the end of that event or after extended exposure; we make rapid judgments that do not change even after extended contact. Some might argue that these rapid judgments should be trusted, and others would say that we should try to suspend the initial judgment and allow more evidence to be assembled through a longer conversation and more data gathering before making a decision. In *Blink,* Malcolm Gladwell argues that "decisions made very quickly can be every bit as good as decisions made cautiously and deliberately." But, ". . . we have to acknowledge the subtle influences that can alter or undermine or bias the products of our unconscious."[1] Structuring the interview process provides some protection against the possible bias in our unconscious judgments.

The Logistics of Preliminary Interviews

Preliminary interviews require substantial orchestration. If you are working without a consultant, you should plan to invest considerable time in the planning and logistics of these visits.

Many preliminary interviews are held in airport hotels because of the convenience for candidates arriving by plane. Hotels can be costly but, by contrast with corporate offices or campuses, they are usually equipped to provide the necessary meeting space, meals, and overnight accommodations, as well as some confidentiality. Some committees use the corporate offices of board members or of the search firm. Use of campus meeting places is usually the lowest-cost alternative and has the advantage of showing the candidates the attractions of the institution. But if the campus is far from the airport, holding preliminary interviews on campus can create logistical burdens. Interviews on campus may also breach the candidate's confidentiality, unless they are held in an area of the campus where they are not likely to be seen by anyone who will recognize them, or by the media.

An hour or perhaps 1½ hours is usually enough for a preliminary interview. Committees sometimes feel that they have so many questions to ask that they must have a longer interview, but in my experience, even the liveliest candidate and the most committed and engaged committee members have a hard time sustaining an interesting conversation for that long. The information gained rarely justifies the time spent much beyond 90 minutes. A candidate whose preliminary interview is successful and whose references are positive will be invited back for an additional interview at which conversations can take place in greater depth.

Questions to Ask in Interviews

The goal of a preliminary interview is to allow the search committee to predict how candidates would perform on the job if they were selected. Research on the predictive value of interviews suggests that the best results are obtained when interviewers use a structured and consistent set of questions, and that those questions should focus on what candidates have done, rather than on what they would do if appointed.[2] If the approach to questions is speculative rather than focused on previous behavior, answers depend more on the ability to generate ideas and present them in an impressive fashion than on the ability to work effectively in a concrete and constrained reality. Although committee members often want to ask, "What *would you do* if you came to our institution?" the better approach is to ask, "What *have you done?*"

Committee members often want to ask candidates, "What is your vision for our institution?" I would suggest beginning with the question, "Would you tell us about a position you have held in which you were expected to articulate a vision? How did you do that?" You can continue, then, with "What might be your vision for _____ College?" One of the dilemmas for candidates in responding to this question is that even the most visionary candidates may want to reserve judgment until they know your institution better. Committee members may view this response as evasive, but it can also be interpreted as showing respect for an inclusive process of engaging the campus in deliberation about its future. By contrast, the candidate who responds by articulating a vision for your campus might be seen by some as a bold and creative thinker, but might also be seen as bringing an agenda and imposing it on others. Laying out a vision of greatness may energize the committee, but that vision is not necessarily achievable. For all these reasons, if the committee asks a question about vision, responses should be interpreted with caution.

Asking a consistent set of questions of all candidates also provides the committee with a set of comparable responses. If some presidential candidates but not all are asked about, for example, how they have worked with local government and community leaders, it will be more difficult to evaluate them on this element of external relations during the process of reviewing candidates after the interviews, leaving the committee frustrated in its efforts.

Interviews lasting one hour or a little more, and allowing time for candidate questions, can usually cover 10–15 questions. As you plan these questions, think carefully about what you said you were looking for in the new president or vice president. If you are looking for someone eager to build relationships with donors and potential donors, ask about experience in that area. If you are looking for someone to restore high morale and enhance communication, ask about experience with that. Be sure that you get the answers to candidate-specific questions, such as the reasons for a series of early departures from previous positions, or an explanation for a campus controversy or a downturn in enrollment. If issues such as these are committee concerns, it is very important not to pass over them; find a way to ask the question that is respectful but direct. Throughout the interview, no matter how lively the conversation and how vivid the responses, you will not remember what candidates said unless you write it down. It is essential that you use a format that encourages committee members to take notes.

Interviews as Opportunities for Recruiting

The active efforts that began the recruiting process come to the fore again during the interviews. Committees are usually well aware that the preliminary interview is an opportunity to screen candidates and put aside those who are not of further interest. But committees should also remember that interviews are for recruiting. Some of your strongest candidates may initially have only a modest interest in the position that you are filling. They may be in other searches that are more attractive, or they may be considering attractive counteroffers from their current institution. The committee should want every single candidate interviewed to leave the room more interested in your position than they were before, and eager to move forward in your search process. You want all the candidates to leave thinking highly of your institution and to tell others what a positive experience they had participating in your search. Most important, you want to be certain that the candidates you like, also like you. What makes a preliminary interview a successful *recruiting* event?

- *Offer hospitality beyond the interview:* Select an attractive location for the interviews; try to accommodate candidates' scheduling concerns; provide assistance with getting from the airport to the interview site (e.g., if taxis in your city are unreliable or poorly maintained, arrange for a car service or for someone from the institution to do airport pickups); phone the candidates in their hotel rooms after they arrive to answer questions or attend to any problems before the interview.

- *Offer hospitality within the interview:* Offer a glass of water or a cup of coffee, and be sure the drink left behind by the previous candidate has been removed; be sure that all committee members introduce themselves and provide table-tents with committee members' names so that the candidate does not have to remember who is who.

- *Structure interview groups that are not too large:* If your search committee has more than 10 members, consider structuring it into smaller groups that can provide a more comfortable setting for conversation. If you take this approach, be sure that all committee members meet all candidates.

- *Show respect in the content of the interview:* Provide sufficient time for candidates to ask their questions of you, and show interest in responding to those questions, even if you have already decided that you are not interested in this candidate. Avoid illegal questions about age, ethnicity, sexual orientation, marital and family status, etc. Attempt to generate a relaxed and conversational tone, even though you are moving systematically through a series of prepared questions.

- *Notify candidates promptly of the decision:* At the end of the interviews, the search chair or the consultant should contact everyone who was interviewed to let them know if they are being asked to move to the next step in the search process. Although it can take substantial time, I think that people who are interviewed personally should be contacted personally, by phone, rather than by e-mail or letter. If that is not possible, the more important issue is to respond promptly; candidates are wondering and often worrying about your decision and you should let them know as soon as you can.

- *Try to provide feedback:* Some candidates who are not being pursued further will thank you for your call and end the conversation, but others will want feedback; the caller should think in advance about what constructive feedback can be offered to each candidate. The way these final conversations are held will shape the unsuccessful candidate's view of you, the institution, and the search process; ideally, every candidate should say, "I had a valuable conversation after the interview that gave me good feedback and made me feel well treated, even though I didn't move forward in the search process."

The Role of the Appointing Officer in the Preliminary Interview

Another significant element of recruiting in the preliminary interview is providing candidates with an opportunity to meet key people. For presidential searches, this is normally the board chair; for vice presidential searches, it is the president. Every candidate's level of interest will be influenced by perceptions of the person to whom they would report. Having the board chair or president participate in the preliminary interviews can go a long way toward successfully recruiting candidates—especially if that person is an appealing character.

If the board chair or president is willing to participate in one or two full days of airport interviews, there are various ways to structure participation. Sometimes this person, who is not normally part of the search committee, simply participates in the committee interviews. This has the advantage of allowing the chair or president to observe the candidates interacting with others, as well as asking one or two of his or her own questions. But there are several disadvantages: the appointing officer may dominate the conversation and distract attention from the questions of other participants, and the format may limit the candidate's opportunity to get an impression of the chair or president because that person is mixed into a larger group. A second alternative is to ask the chair or president to interview all these candidates individually. This is easy enough to structure; for example, the committee can meet for an hour with the first candidate while the chair or president meets with the second candidate, switching after an hour. Although this can be more challenging to arrange and manage, it allows a mutual personal appraisal to occur, and it gives the chair or president an opportunity to persuade the candidates of the attractiveness of the institution and the position.

The committee should also consider whether and how to include the chair or president in the committee's debriefing meeting. Some committees will prefer to deliberate and select preferred candidates without nonmember input. Others will reason that there is no point pursuing a candidate with whom the president or board chair does not want to work.

If the chair or president joins the airport interviews, a great deal of their time will be invested in talking to candidates who are deselected immediately afterward. Some chairs and presidents may think that this is not a good use of their time. A chair or president who is unable or unwilling to participate in the preliminary interviews should definitely find time for a substantial conversation with the candidates who are selected for further review, either by phone or in person during the second-round interviews.

Narrowing the Candidate Pool and Selecting Finalists

At the conclusion of the preliminary interviews, the committee should allow a couple of hours for debriefing and decision making about which candidates should move to the next step in the search process. This discussion immediately after the interviews allows the committee to capture impressions that are fresh, comparing notes and formulating a sense of the strengths and limitations that each candidate would bring. The chair will want to lead this meeting carefully, and might encourage committee members to continue using the rating sheet that was used for the initial screening of candidate files (see Appendix H). The approach should be to discuss each candidate's strengths and weaknesses systematically. Each committee member should have the chance to be heard and to ask questions of others. If a candidate is uniformly seen as weak, it is not necessary to discuss him or her in detail, although there should be enough discussion so that the person phoning the candidate with the bad news has a few words to offer about strengths and weaknesses.

There are several pitfalls in the debriefing meeting that follow the preliminary interviews:

- Some committees have a tendency to move directly into a comparative framework, e.g., "I liked Jane's approach to fund-raising better than Joan's, but I liked Joan's approach to strategic planning better than Jean's." Beginning with a comparative approach does not give each candidate a fair appraisal; it is better to begin by discussing one candidate at a time. A comparative approach can also be confusing to participants and lead to misunderstanding, e.g., "Were you referring to Mark or Max when you said the candidate was too soft-spoken? Was Mark the one with the striped tie or the paisley tie?" Some committees might wish to reduce the risk of confusion by using photos of candidates; however, this approach also increases the risk of discrimination and should be avoided.

- Some committees have one or two very articulate and outspoken members whose early expression of their views can swamp open discussion—for instance, "Well, obviously, we won't be pursuing Bill!" Those who saw strengths in Bill should have the opportunity to make their case.

- Especially when there are internal candidates, committee members may be reluctant to express their views. The interview debriefing meeting should begin with yet another reminder about confidentiality.

Considering the Fragile Candidate Pool

Committees often ask how many candidates should be advanced after the preliminary interview to the next step, which is normally additional reference checking. In most searches, six or seven is a good number, allowing for the possibility that a few will have less impressive reference reports, and that three to five candidates will then continue on to second-round interviews. However, there are some searches in which the candidate pool is fragile. By this I mean that it is a pool from which several candidates could easily be lost, and the committee could risk ending up with none to consider. For example, one candidate might be under consideration in several searches, one might be likely to get a counteroffer from his or her own institution, one might have family considerations that create reluctance to make the move at this time, and one might have compensation needs that push the limits of what the institution can provide. There may also be institutional features that will make it hard to persuade the preferred candidate to accept the appointment, such as budget deficits, enrollment shortfalls, or a divided board. If the pool is fragile, the committee should move more candidates to the next step in the process rather than fewer. Consider identifying alternates in case one or more people decline your invitation to move forward in the search.

STEP 10: REFERENCE CALLS AND BACKGROUND CHECKS

Checking references is an absolutely essential part of the search process. Mistakes are often made at this point, or corners are cut, and institutions later discover these flaws in the search process that led to errors in hiring. Invest the time and effort in contacting enough references and asking probing questions, and then pay attention to what you are told.

There are many ways to approach references in executive searches—but using letters of reference is not one of them! Although many committee members who have participated in faculty searches and mid-level management searches will expect to use letters of reference, they are not well suited to presidential and vice presidential searches. Letters of reference are not attuned to the particular nature of your institution and the expectations of your position. They may omit important information. And they do not permit you to explore in depth the particular issues you are interested in or areas of concern you have identified. If you receive a letter of reference from an important source of information about your candidate (e.g., the candidate's board chair), you may want to speak by phone with that reference as well.

The Timing of Reference Calls

References may be checked at various points in the search. Sometimes a few references are checked as part of the initial screening process, before extending invitations to preliminary interviews. Sometimes references are called while you are waiting for the preliminary interviews to occur so that during the debriefing at the conclusion of these interviews, reference information can also be reviewed and taken into account as the finalists are being selected. And sometimes references are checked after the preliminary interviews but before selecting finalists, or even after finalists have been selected. Each approach has advantages and disadvantages. The selection of one over the other may depend as much on schedule constraints as on preferences.

If the search schedule permits, my preference is to make early reference calls during the screening phase if I have a concern about a candidate; this allows reference reports to shape the decision of which candidates to interview. I make the majority of reference calls to listed references right after the preliminary interviews. The reason for calling after the interviews is that, having met the candidate, the reference call can address any concerns that emerged in the interview. Calling references after the preliminary interviews also avoids a lot of calls to candidates whose interviews are unsuccessful. This saves work for those making the reference calls, but it also protects the references from extra work and the candidate from confidentiality risks and potential embarrassment if they do not move forward in the search.

Many candidates are reluctant or even unwilling to grant permission to call references at an early stage of the search. Your calls to references entail burden for those called as well as increased risk of breached confidentiality for the candidates. This reluctance typically extends especially to calls to individuals who are not listed as references. So a committee's timetable for reference calls has to be adapted to the candidate's willingness to grant permission for those calls. The issue of obtaining permission for reference calls is discussed in greater detail below.

Questions to Ask References

When committee members make reference calls, it is a good idea to agree in advance on what questions will be asked and what approach will be taken. (See Appendix I for suggested reference questions.) The questions you ask should be linked to the qualifications you have specified for the position. For example, if fund-raising is the primary focus of the president's role, you will want to talk to people who have worked closely with your candidate on fund-raising, perhaps planning donor development strategy, or attending alumni events and entertaining prospective donors, or actually making solicitation visits. You will want to ask references questions that give you a good understanding of what the candidate has actually done, and you will hope to gain confidence that the candidate has had sufficient successful experience in fund-raising to move effectively into the presidency of your institution. You should ask whether the candidate seems to like fund-raising or if it is seen as a burdensome responsibility. If you are searching for a chief financial officer who must deal with an extremely complex and constrained budget, you will want to ask about experience with that kind of situation, the ability to craft creative but appropriate budgetary strategies, the ability to discuss the budget with those who do not have finance expertise, any history of problems in the area of financial management, and so on.

There are cases when a standardized reference format is not as useful. There may be candidates who have raised concerns in your mind—concerns about an apparently premature departure from another institution, or series of situations in which things did not go as expected, or a vote of no confidence. The search committee will have to understand the situation and determine whether it reflects badly on the candidate, or if the candidate learned from it, or was in fact the source of the problem and is likely to carry that problem with him or her to future positions. In these cases, I recommend allowing the reference to tell the story that you need to hear in a more free-form way. In a presidential search, for example, I might ask a candidate's reference to tell me why the candidate stepped down from his or her previous position while looking for another position. I might say, "Did you try to convince him to stay?" Or, "How would you compare this person to the person you subsequently hired into this position?" If there was a significant campus controversy, I might ask the reference to tell me the story of the controversy and simply follow the story as it is told. Do not be afraid to ask the questions about issues that are of concern to you, even though they may be uncomfortable (e.g., "Was he fired?"); that is the point of the reference call.

Assigning Reference Calls

Thought should be given to assigning the reference calls; it is almost always an advantage for references to be called by people they know or people who are their peers or at least in similar areas of responsibility (a dean would call a dean, a board member would call a board member or another member of the external community, and so on). It is preferable to spread the calls for each candidate among several committee members. This has the advantage of avoiding the loyalty that a committee member may develop toward that candidate who may become "my candidate" simply because that committee member made the reference calls. This loyalty can blind the caller to concerns raised in the reference conversation. Committee members making the calls may be unequally skilled, and using several different callers overcomes this limitation.

If you are working with a search consultant, you will find that some make all the reference calls, whereas others engage committee members in making the calls. Either approach can work well. The choice depends on the culture of the committee and the preferences of the consultant. Consultants are experienced at making reference calls, although some tend to push harder to uncover potential flaws while others are more focused on identifying strengths. Having the consultant make all the calls reduces the burden on the committee members, and adds consistency to the reports. However, when consultants make all the calls, committee members receive all reference information secondhand, through the lens the consultant uses.

Permission to Call Listed References

You should always obtain the permission of candidates before making reference calls. This is a matter of courtesy, and in some institutions it is a matter of policy. It is also a practical matter, allowing candidates to notify their references to expect a call and to describe the position to them and the reason for their interest in it. It is a matter of confidentiality; candidates take a significant step when they allow you to begin to call their references, and they should be aware of the risks to keeping their interest confidential. Candidates can sometimes feel abused by the reference-checking process. If it is done improperly, the candidate may withdraw from your search or be reluctant to enter other searches for fear of similar mistreatment.

When you are making reference calls for six or seven candidates, you will normally only be able to obtain permission to call those people who are listed as references. If you feel the list of references is not adequate, you might ask for more names or certain kinds of names to be added to the list. For example, committees often want the opportunity to talk to students, or a staff member in the candidate's office, or a donor, but candidates do not always include these kinds of people on their reference lists. Appendix B suggests the kinds of names that should be included on a reference list; candidates whose reference lists do not seem adequate can be asked to review these suggestions and provide additional reference names.

Some people assume that anyone who is listed as a reference by a candidate will be completely enthusiastic; this is simply not true. You may have to dig a little deeper and listen a little harder, but it is remarkable how many candidates list as references people who are not fully supportive of them. I have even had a listed reference say, "I really don't know why he lists me as a reference. I have nothing good to say about him."

Permission to Call Those Not Listed as References

Once your candidate pool is narrowed to between three and five candidates, you will want to ask candidates for permission to call people who are not on their reference lists. Most candidates will agree to this step, although some will with-hold permission to call certain kinds of people (e.g., you may be asked not to call anyone at the candidate's current institution, or not to call his or her current supervisor or board chair). In the extreme case, a candidate will say that you may not call a particular person (most often the current supervisor) unless an offer has been made. From the perspective of the consultant or committee, accepting this stipulation is a very risky strategy. Once an offer has been extended, there is a certain momentum that makes it difficult to change direc-tion if the reference reveals serious problems. It is actually a risky strategy from the candidate's perspective too; restricting access to a key person raises the con-cern that this person is going to say something that may be damaging. Some-times the reason for the restriction is understandable. For example, there are some presidents who treat interest in another position on the part of their vice presidents as a sign of disloyalty, and this president will distrust the candidate from then on, or may even dismiss him or her.

In every search, it is essential to make calls to some people who were not listed as references. Candidates who balk at off-list reference calls at the finalist stage of the search, after they have had an open second-round interview, are being unrealistic about the confidentiality of the search process. If there is no on-campus interview in which a broad institutional audience participates, it may be possible to maintain confidentiality until the final selection is made. But if there has been an on-campus interview, the national network of faculty and others can be expected to be activated instantly, with people e-mailing and calling friends and colleagues at the candidate's institution to check on their performance.

Pitfalls in Checking References

The reference-checking process has pitfalls and can be flawed, even fatally flawed, leading you to make a serious hiring mistake. Checking too few referen-ces is a common problem, often caused by rushing this stage of the process. I find that it usually takes about three weeks to complete a full set of references. Can-didates take a few days to provide the kinds of references that you are looking for, and it may take them a few more days to notify these people that they may receive a call. Calls are placed to reach the references but not all are easily avail-able; some are traveling and unable to schedule a call with you for a week or more. Once callers have completed the reference conversation, they should write up a report on each reference so that it can be circulated to other commit-tee members. Allow enough time for these steps so that enough references can be completed.

Another potential flaw in checking references, or even in evaluating the refer-ences checked by others, is hearing only what you want to hear. There may be candidates whose written materials are so strong, and whose interview was so compelling, that you are counting on the reference to confirm the appraisal you have already made. Sometimes this creeps into the formulation of your questions. ("Everyone seems to think Ann is a great person, and I guess you do too, don't you?) Sometimes it leads you to disregard red flags in the references comments. (Listen carefully if you hear the reference say, "I think Bob was a very successful president here, but of course not everyone would agree with that.") Be vigilant and disciplined in your reading of the reference reports so that you recognize any red flags that may be there.

Dealing with Negative References

What should you do when you hear negative comments in a reference? You should pursue the area of concern, with this reference and with others, until you are satisfied as to whether or not it is a problem for your search. Many times, the negatives in references reflect problems that would likely be repeated in future positions. The reference may say, for example, "As provost, this person never saw a decision that he didn't prefer to refer to a committee." If this approach is alien to a hard-driving board of trustees, this candidate is probably not someone you want to select as president. You might want to confirm this appraisal with others at the institution, but you should not expect this trait to disappear in a new environment. But there are some institutions in which relatively slow decision making is seen as appropriate reflectiveness, and in which the creation of committees is seen as inclusive shared governance. By contrast, you may hear that a candidate is viewed as autocratic, rarely seeking input as he implements a personal vision that is not shared by many on the campus. Again, there may be some institutions in which this is exactly the kind of leadership the board is seeking in a new president. A reference may offer a more general observation, such as "He will be a great provost if he has learned the lessons of his previous mistakes." That kind of elliptical comment should be pursued to learn what the mistakes were and what lessons should have been learned.

Having described the red flags that should raise serious concerns, I should also say that some problems you uncover probably should be put aside and not treated as major concerns. Critical comments about candidates can come from listed or off-list references, but of course they are more likely to be heard when you talk to people who are not listed as references. I often ask candidates to provide me with a list of their critics, on the grounds that everyone who has done anything as an administrator will have critics. A candidate might respond to this question by explaining why a particular colleague is a critic, and offering his or her own perspective on the situation (e.g., "I felt that this dean had staffing levels that were appropriate to a higher level of enrollment than the school was able to attract, but the dean was resentful of the budget cuts I made"). Or you may hear criticism about a candidate's approach in an institutional context that is very different from yours and decide that it will not be a problem in your institution. For example, a dean who worked quietly and respectfully with faculty might be seen as a poor performer in an institution where the president and provost were hard-charging, but in an environment in which healing is needed, that dean might make a very effective provost.

Evaluating Reference Reports

All reference reports should not be given equal weight. Some references are so effusive that it is impossible to tell what the candidate's real achievements have been, and what is fluff. Some references are curmudgeons who are never satisfied. They may claim that the provost did not listen, but you may decide that actually the provost listened and decided not to take that person's advice. Some references are not well informed, having never worked with the candidate on a daily basis and knowing the candidate's accomplishments and approach only as a result of what the candidate himself or herself has said. A consultant who has talked with references for various candidates over the years can help to sort out which comments tell you about the candidate, and which reveal more about the person providing the reference. There are also some extraordinary references who have an exceptional ability to grasp a candidate's strengths, weaknesses, and readiness for the next move, and will tell you that frankly. These references are enormously valuable.

Evaluating Scholarly and Creative Work

At some institutions and for some positions, the quality of scholarly or creative work must be evaluated with particular care. This is normally the responsibility of the faculty members on the search committee. They may wish to review these items themselves, or may seek the appraisal of others in the same field or specialty area as the candidate. In order to protect the confidentiality of candidates, these consultations may be postponed until a later stage in the search.

Background Checks

In addition to the reference calls that are made for candidates, you should do background checks on your finalists. The more you narrow your pool of candidates, the deeper the background checks should be. You will probably want to verify educational credentials for the top 10, but may only check criminal or credit record for the final three, partly because of the intrusion entailed by these checks, and partly because fees are charged by the companies that carry out these searches. The key items in background checks are searching Web databases, verifying academic credentials, verifying employment, and checking criminal record, credit record, driving record, military record, and litigation. Normally these reports are not shared with the committee, but the chair should review them and determine whether there are areas of concern of which the committee needs to be aware.

The search chair should be certain that a Web search has been done for each candidate, and often committee members will do these searches as well. Using a search engine or Lexis-Nexis (a database of newspapers) to learn more about the candidates can be exceptionally revealing but can also create problems. One of these problems is the variable standard of accuracy. Candidates who have been active leaders are not always popular with all their constituencies. Sometimes those who do not like what the candidate has done can get public attention for their point of view, and as a result the Web search reveals critical press reports or hostile blogs. But often the candidate who holds a senior administrative position is not able to tell the story publicly from his or her own perspective, and thus the press reports or blogs are one-sided. The search committee should consider this possibility and, if the candidate is someone in whom you are otherwise interested, ask him or her to explain the situation, or ask a reference to explain it.

In the corporate world, search processes may include psychological tests, administered either by the company's human resources office or by an outside firm. These tests are rarely used in higher education.

STEP 11: SECOND-ROUND INTERVIEWS
Selecting Candidates for Second-Round Interviews

Selecting candidates for second-round interviews is a critical decision. The committee has before it a substantial body of information about each candidate: the candidate's letter and CV, the results of the preliminary interview, the reference reports, and background checks.

At this meeting, the references are normally the focus of attention because they offer new information from those who actually know and have worked with the candidates. The references may alleviate concerns—e.g., "I understand why you would ask about whether Sue is a good listener. I remember that when we interviewed Sue she seemed to talk more than she listened, but as I have worked with her over the last five years, I have to say that she is extremely open to others' ideas and everyone feels she listens carefully to their concerns. So I think you don't have to be worried about whether she is a good listener." The references may also raise new concerns. ("Mike left our institution under circumstances that none of us quite understands. Although he moved to another vice presidency at a prominent institution, you should probably talk to our board chair about why he was not selected to be our president last year.") The positive and negative references may both be about the same candidate, and the committee will thus have difficult decisions to make.

As the committee selects a small group of candidates for second-round interviews, what is the right number of candidates to invite? Few institutions are comfortable with bringing only one candidate. Committees want and need points of comparison and a sense that they have a real choice. Two is also often seen as too few. Typically three to five candidates are selected, depending on the quality of the candidate pool and the campus policy or tradition for number of finalists. I would view five candidates as an absolute maximum; if more than five candidates are brought back, the burden on the campus is substantial, and you may lose some candidates who feel that their chances of success are too low to justify the demands of the process. The most common number of finalists is probably three. The committee may identify alternates in case the candidates they invite are not available or decline the invitation.

Structuring the Second-Round Interviews—Open vs. Closed

The second-round interviews are a very significant moment in the search. At that point, you are gaining far deeper knowledge about a narrower group of people. Conversations will be more exploratory and probing and less scripted. A wider group of people will meet each candidate and each interviewer or group will provide feedback to the search committee or the appointing officer, significantly broadening your understanding of the candidate. The interview will occur over a more extended period of time, and the candidate can be seen at times of high energy and after a long and exhausting series of conversations, in informal conversations and formal presentations, in less guarded moments as you walk between meetings, and over meals.

There are two general approaches to second-round interviews. They can be open and public events, held on campus, with all members of the campus community invited to participate and media present at some of the events. Or, second-round interviews can be kept relatively closed and confidential, including only the search committee, the appointing officer, and perhaps a carefully selected small group of additional participants. Candidates often balk at the idea of second-round interviews that are open and public. Consider whether you want to risk losing strong candidates, especially in a presidential search, by insisting on full public exposure and the associated loss of confidentiality. Insisting on open interviews can weaken the quality of the candidate pool if strong candidates withdraw for this reason.

Open second-round interviews are the usual choice among public institutions, and especially in "sunshine" states in which virtually all of the search process may have to be public. But many private institutions take this approach as well. It has both advantages and disadvantages.

Advantages of open second-round interviews:

- The primary advantage of open second-round interviews is precisely that they are open. Faculty, staff, and students at institutions with a tradition of shared governance will expect to have an opportunity to meet all finalists and will be seriously alarmed if they do not. The controversy over this matter can be extreme, normally focusing on the need for campus input into this very important decision. Some campuses may understand that insisting on public interviews can lead to a weaker pool of candidates and a weaker appointment, and some will give up their claim to participate in the interest of strengthening the pool. But other campuses will not accept this, arguing that any candidate who does not want an open campus interview is not a candidate they would want.

- There are some advantages for candidates in open interviews. Candidates who place an especially high value on shared governance will want to give all campus constituencies an opportunity to participate in the process. In addition, candidates who want to get a feel for the campus culture and the tone and morale of faculty, staff, and students before deciding whether or not to accept the position will want substantial firsthand exposure. Thus, open interviews offer an opportunity for candidates to decide for themselves if this position is a good fit.

- Open interviews bring the input of a wide range of individuals and groups, and the appointing officer can gain valuable information from this input. If the deans and department chairs have serious objections to one of the candidates for chief financial officer, some presidents will feel that this candidate is not viable—although the president seeking change in the approach to resource allocation and accountability may feel this is just the right person to appoint! In either case, the feedback provides valuable information that might be missed if only a select group met the finalists.

- Bringing a diverse group of candidates for open interviews offers real choices and the opportunity for diversification of the senior leadership, and of course it also sends a message to the campus. If all the finalists are white males, it will be more difficult to convince future search committees that diversity is important. But if there are women and people of color in the finalist pool of a majority institution, a different conclusion can be drawn. Most important, the strength of diversity candidates can offer the opportunity for a diversity appointment.

Disadvantages of open second-round interviews:

- Candidates whose current positions are especially visible or vulnerable, or who are content in their current jobs and unwilling to be publicly known as a candidate, may decline to participate in a public interview process. If your preferred candidate withdraws from the search because he or she is unwilling to have a public interview, your candidate pool is weakened—perhaps fatally so, if you do not have other strong finalists. This disadvantage is the context within which all other advantages and disadvantages should be seen.

- Open interviews exacerbate the hazard created by having a large number of finalists (four or more). For example, if you are bringing three finalists to campus, candidates will calculate their odds of success at one in three and most will be willing to participate. But if you are bringing five or six candidates to campus, the odds drop and a candidate may withdraw because the risks associated both with the number of candidates and the public exposure outweigh the potential gain.

- Exposing candidates to all constituencies opens the possibility of a divided or politicized final selection process, with associated bad publicity and harm to the reputation of the search and of the institution. Faculty may line up behind one candidate while the board may prefer another. Students may lobby vocally and visibly for or against a particular candidate.

- Open interviews create challenges when there are internal candidates, and especially if the person in the interim position is a finalist. For example, you will need to determine whether the internal candidate is invited to meet the outside candidates and permitted to attend their presentations or meetings with them.

- A series of open interviews is very taxing for a campus, not to mention the burden for the staff charged with arranging the schedules. You do not want to subject your colleagues to this burden unnecessarily.

- Open interviews create the illusion that the final selection is the domain of one campus constituency (typically the faculty) or of all campus constituencies, rather than being the decision of the president or the board. Using closed interviews makes it more clear whose decision this is.

Closed second-round interviews are the alternative to public second-round interviews. If this approach is taken, there may be a second round of conversations just with the search committee, just with the appointing officer, or (in a hybrid approach) with a slightly and carefully expanded group that is as committed to confidentiality as the search committee has been. That group can include the leaders of the faculty, staff, and student governance groups, additional representatives of the major organizational units (e.g., all the vice presidents or deans, or one additional faculty member from each school within the institution), or an expanded group of board members for a presidential appointment. Again, there are advantages and disadvantages of each approach.

Advantages of closed second-round interviews:

- The greatest advantage of the closed second-round interview is the greater strength of the candidates who are likely to be attracted to the search if protection from public events is provided. The promise of confidentiality until the appointment is announced reduces risk for candidates and can cause otherwise reluctant but strong candidates to consider entering the search process.

- The closed interview may provide for greater candor in feedback, and for greater opportunity to probe responses from participants. When there are hundreds of participants, many will offer no feedback. When there are only a dozen or two, everyone can share observations, and this may provide more valuable information about potential effectiveness to the board or president.

- Managing closed interviews is less burdensome than managing open interviews. And the process is less burdensome for all participants, without the wine-and-cheese receptions, ferrying of candidates from one location to another, media interviews, or media avoidance.

Disadvantages of closed second-round interviews:

- The primary disadvantage of closed interviews is precisely that they are closed. They have a feeling of being shrouded in secrecy—not normally a welcome approach, especially on a college or university campus. Some institutional representatives are invited to participate and some are not. This is almost always publicly controversial, privately hurtful, or both. Closed interviews are likely to exclude some people who could provide valuable input if they were invited, but who are not invited because of the pressure to keep the participant list relatively short.

- The disadvantage for candidates is that they have no opportunity to get the sense of the campus as a whole—the people, the issues, the climate. They may wonder whether the participants in the closed interviews were handpicked to exclude dissenters, or to keep from view the disruptive and demoralized individuals with whom any new president or vice president will have to deal. Although interviews always have some artificiality, closed interviews may feel more artificial because they are more controlled than open interviews.

The open-vs.-closed issue is a difficult one. Some institutions will treat this as a policy decision. Others will respond to past practices; because the previous presidential search had closed interviews, it is generally expected that the current search will also have closed interviews, or there may be a long-standing expectation that all executive searches have open second-round interviews. Others will treat the choice situationally; in early phases of the search, the campus can be made aware that a decision about open interviews will depend on the impact of an open format on the strength of the candidate pool; if candidates are willing, the interviews will be open, but if they are unwilling and may otherwise withdraw from the search, the interviews will be closed.

Participation in Second-Round Interviews

Once the decision is made as to whether the second-round interviews should be open or closed, that decision has to be implemented. There are two underlying considerations: (1) include those whose input will be useful in the evaluation of candidates; and (2) include those who can help to recruit candidates by providing them with the information they need in order to decide whether to accept the position if it is offered. Often, unfortunately, second-round interviews are planned with only the first consideration in mind.

For open interviews, each institution will craft a schedule appropriate to its particular situation, but a typical itinerary for candidates would include the following:

- *Trustees:* In a presidential search, as many trustees as possible should meet the finalists. In fact, all trustees are normally invited to participate but not all may be able to do so. Trustees should have a variety of settings in which to get to know candidates, including group and individual interviews, formal presentations by the candidates, and social settings to which spouses or partners are invited.

  In a vice presidential search, the president and board chair will normally decide who should participate depending on the role that the bylaws assign to trustees in the process of appointing vice presidents. Typical trustee participants would be the chair or members of the executive committee and the chair or members of the committee that works most closely with the vice president being appointed (e.g., a search for the vice president for advancement would normally invite the chair of the board's advancement committee and capital campaign committee).

- *Senior officers:* In a presidential search, there may not be any vice presidents on the search committee, reflecting the view held by some that no one should participate in the selection of the person to whom they will report, especially if not all the direct reports can participate. But at the finalist stage, all vice presidents can be invited and, unless they do not have the confidence of the board or the outgoing president, their opinions should be taken especially seriously. They have the best collective sense of the issues of the campus and the expectations of the presidency, and will be able both to judge the candidates from these perspectives and to tell the candidates about institutional issues. As with all participants in the interview process, their enthusiasm and insights can help to recruit reluctant candidates. Meeting the vice presidents also allows candidates to get at least a preliminary sense of whether the new president will inherit a smoothly functioning team that has apparent compatibility with the candidate's approach to leadership, or whether senior-level housecleaning will be needed promptly.

  In a vice presidential search, there is typically a meeting with the other vice presidents, and with the outgoing VP. The group of vice presidents can make an appraisal of whether the candidate will be a good fit. As with a presidential search, they can both evaluate the candidates, inform the candidates, and help with the effort to recruit reluctant candidates.

  Because resources are essential to institutional health and success, it is extremely important for candidates to meet with those who are responsible for revenue. This would normally include the senior officers for enrollment, advancement, and finance. The committee should decide how best to structure these conversations; the crucial point is that candidates must gain a very clear understanding of what the resources are and the key constraints upon them.

  If the outgoing person was in some way forced to leave the position, or if the outgoing person is an interim appointee who is also a candidate for the position, there are special considerations in planning the interview. Candidates are always eager to meet the person who has held the position most recently, since this person is normally the best source of information about the realities of the position. The search committee may fear that someone who is departing unhappily may poison the thinking of candidates, telling them the worst parts of the job. I find that this rarely happens and that, when it does, the committee can usually anticipate this and prepare the candidates by providing a context for what they are likely to hear.

- *Internal candidates and interim appointees:* Normally, the interim appointee would participate in this phase of the interview process. However, if that person is also a candidate for the position, he or she would not participate in the interviews. Interim appointees who were candidates at an earlier stage in the process but have been dropped from further consideration pose a different set of concerns. In this situation, I sometimes talk with the interim appointee about his or her preferences. There is a wide range of workable approaches. The interim person might arrange to be off campus for the day of the interview to avoid all contact; or might decide to "meet and greet" candidates as a courtesy, but not to spend any interview time with them; or might meet with the candidates as part of a group but not individually; or might fully participate in the interview process as though they had never been a candidate. Interim appointees who want to stay on at the institution and thus need to get on well with their successor may take one approach. Interim appointees who feel that, having been rejected, they must now leave, are likely to take another approach. There is no formula for addressing this circumstance; the arrangements should respond to the specific elements of the situation and the individuals involved.

- *Deans and directors:* The participation of deans and directors will be most extensive for those most closely linked organizationally to the appointee. In an open interview, this group might have a special session with candidates, and in a closed interview there should be some representation. For example, in a CFO search, the directors of units closely linked to finance, and the associate deans whose portfolios include budget, will especially need to be involved. With an open interview, all could be invited. With a closed interview, one of them might represent the perspective of the others.

- *Faculty and faculty leaders:* Faculty are typically a critical audience (in both senses) for finalist interviews. They are normally a powerful force in the selection process. Even trustees who are far removed from the daily flow of events on campus are often well aware that the new president or vice president needs to have good working relationships with the faculty. Strong and widespread opposition to a candidate will in many cases weaken if not end the candidacy. It is often said that faculty have highly honed critical thinking skills that make them likely to find flaws in any situation, proposal, or person. For whatever reason, the faculty is often the hardest audience to please.

    Elected and appointed faculty leaders (e.g., senate officers, department chairs) are typically key participants in the open interview process. In some cases they may be given time alone with each candidate, and in other cases they will be especially encouraged to participate as part of a larger group. Conversations with the faculty during an open interview process can be organized in various ways. A typical approach is to schedule an open forum at which the candidate is asked to introduce himself or herself and to speak for 10 or 15 minutes on a particular topic, such as the most significant issues facing higher education in the coming decade, or the issues facing this sector of higher education (e.g., public research universities, or small private liberal arts colleges). This allows the audience to see how the candidates speak before an audience, and how they analyze a situation. The presentation would be followed by a question-and-answer period that can focus on the talk, or on any other topics of interest to the audience.

    Sometimes these faculty forums are defined as institutional forums to which staff and students are also invited. Some institutions separate these three groups, either because of the campus's traditions or politics, or because of the concern that the faculty will dominate the discussion and crowd out the voices of the other groups.

    Attendance at faculty forums is sometimes robust and sometimes limited. Limited attendance is an embarrassment. Finding the right time of day for this event can enhance attendance, as can providing refreshments. The lack of participation can mean there is a sense of alienation from the search process, or it can mean that faculty are willing to leave the selection responsibility to someone else. Sometimes it means that there was not enough advance notice. Whatever the cause, the committee and staff to the committee should strive to be sure there is an adequate audience for all candidates.

- *Staff:* If staff are not included in an institution-wide forum, they would normally have one of their own. The approach can be the same as for the faculty forum, described above.

- *Students:* Meetings with students can be powerful elements in the interview process. Students often ask the most revealing questions and can be among the most compelling voices from the perspective of recruiting the reluctant candidate. They can also provide valuable and distinctive responses to a candidate's questions about, for example, why students are attracted to attend this institution, what needs to be improved, and why some leave. Any students on the search committee and student government officers should be asked to take the lead in planning this event. If there is a concern that attendance is likely to be low, encourage personal invitations from student leaders to their peers. Scheduling the event for a small room rather than a large auditorium can reduce the sense of awkwardness if the group is smaller than expected.

- *Alumni:* Alumni take a strong interest in institutional leadership and especially the presidency, and can provide an important base of support for the new president. If there are not enough alumni in the local area likely to participate in a session for alumni alone, they can be invited to sessions to which community members or board members are also invited. But normally the leadership of the alumni association will attend and will encourage others to attend as well.

- *Collective bargaining groups:* Some institutions will want or need to provide special events for the leadership of collective bargaining groups, some will include the leadership of those groups within other sessions (e.g., faculty union officers would participate in the faculty sessions along with their faculty senate colleagues), and some will not recognize unions at all in the interviews. This is a matter of local tradition and politics.

- *Equity and diversity officers and groups:* Those responsible for or especially interested in issues of equity and diversity are often especially interested in executive searches. Some institutions may resist the notion of giving these groups special access to candidates, while others (typically institutions that make diversity issues an especially high priority) are more inclined to do this.

- *Task forces and other groups focused on key institutional issues:* There are often dozens of groups and individuals with special interests who would like to have special access to candidates: the junior faculty and the senior faculty, the athletic director and coaches of major sports, the task force on alcohol and drug issues, and so on. Time constraints and the sense that there is no good way to draw the line between those who are and are not granted special access typically combine to deny these groups the access that they seek. Members of these groups can be encouraged to come to the open forums and raise their questions in that broader setting.

- *External leadership:* Including community leaders and major donors in the interview process can be valuable. While the search committee and board or appointing officer may not normally be as concerned about the preferences of external audiences, there are situations in which these voices are significant. When a campaign is about to be launched, for example, there may be particular interest in how donors respond to the candidates. In a small town, inviting the mayor and the head of the Rotary or Chamber of Commerce can be an important gesture not just in the selection process, but in sending a message of community partnership beyond the search.

With this array of groups and individuals lining up to meet the candidates, the visit for an open interview could last for several days, plus possibly a day of travel before and after the visit. But candidates who have countless other obligations associated with their current positions may find it difficult to break away for such a long time. Campus interviews of one to two days are normal; anything beyond that is unusual.

Closed second-round interviews are typically much shorter, and normally they will last less than one day. A typical schedule would include a second meeting with the search committee, a meeting with as many additional board members as can participate, and a meeting with a select group of campus leaders drawn from the senior staff and the leadership of the faculty, staff, and students.

The Logistics of Second-Round Interviews

The logistics of second-round interviews, whether open or closed, can be very complex, with candidates' spouses or partners and even children sometimes invited and needing special attention. Scheduling interviews can also be challenging. Try to let candidates know as early as possible in the search process which dates are being targeted for the interviews, and as you narrow your pool after the preliminary interviews, remind those candidates going forward of the planned interview dates that they should be holding open in case they are invited to participate in a second round of interviews.

An itinerary for the visit has to be constructed and someone assigned to schedule all participants, reserve rooms, arrange for refreshments and restaurant reservations, assign hosts to get the candidate from one place to another and to make introductions, make hotel reservations and confirm travel itineraries, and on and on. This element of the search process is extremely demanding for the institution, both in terms of staffing and logistics, and in terms of the time and energy of participants in the visit. Needless to say, it is also very demanding for the candidate.

Family Members and the Second-Round Interview

The spouse or partner is normally invited to the second-round interview, and children may be invited as well. There are several underlying themes. It is valuable to cultivate the interest of family members by welcoming them personally to the community, showing them what an attractive community it is, letting them evaluate the job opportunities that they would have if they moved, and seeing the schools and the housing. Moreover, the candidate who is offered the

position will have to decide whether to accept; especially if that involves reloca-
tion, the decision to accept is likely to be a family decision. Inviting family
members to the second-round interview gives them the information they need
to participate in the decision, shortening the time that the selected candidate
will need to decide whether to accept the offer. If the first-choice candidate
takes a long time to make his or her decision, it will be harder to keep the
second-choice candidate waiting, so the institution has an interest in moving
to a prompt decision.

The activities for family members during the second-round interview can
vary. In an open interview, the spouse or partner is normally invited to attend
the large group sessions, such as the open forum at which the candidate makes
a presentation, but not the individual or small-groups meetings. The board will
often want to meet the spouse or partner and can structure an event at which
that is appropriate, e.g., a dinner to which the trustees also bring guests. Other
activities often included are tours of the area with a realtor or visits to the president's house, visits to schools, visits to museums, and other local points of interest. Some presidential spouses or partners have professions that lead them to be
interested in other kinds of meetings. And some may prefer to explore the community on their own.

Feedback from Second-Round Interviews

At the end of the second-round interviews, feedback should be gathered.
Although there are many ways to do this (formally or informally, by phone or
by e-mail, by personal conversations or group meetings), all those who participated in the visit should be given some opportunity to share their observations
with the search committee or appointing officer. A sample campus response
sheet is in Appendix J. The search committee chair should arrange for these
responses to be assembled, tallied, and circulated for members to review and discuss at the final committee meeting.

Calls to Those Not Listed as References

While the second-round interviews are being planned and carried out, a final
round of reference calls should be made. If the second-round interviews are
open, it is likely that many on campus will be making calls to colleagues at the
candidates' institutions, or even cold calls to individuals they do not know to
see what they say about the candidates. If there has been media interest in the
search, reporters may make calls and do Web searches. Committees should have
done enough research of their own that no surprises are uncovered at this stage.

It is very easy as the search moves toward a conclusion to be consumed by the
excitement and the effort of the interviews and to overlook the very important
step of making calls to those who are not listed as references. The management
of these calls is described above in the section on references. The chair or

consultant should keep a watch over these calls to be sure they are made and that reports are brought back to the committee.

STEP 12: THE FINAL DECISION-MAKING PROCESS
Visiting the Candidate's Campus

As the final step in the process approaches, some search committees consider making a visit to the current campus of the finalists. Some view these visits as effective in helping the committee to learn more about the candidates and thus to make a better decision. For example, the search chair and one or two other committee members might travel to the campus and arrange for a series of face-to-face meetings with the candidate's peers, supervisors, and subordinates; might talk with students either in planned meetings or informally on the campus; and may be invited to go to the candidate's home for coffee or a meal. The expectation is that these visits will reveal more than reference calls do about how the candidate works and lives, and how he or she is viewed by others.

But the visits do not always reveal these things accurately. The colleagues of a candidate who is not viewed positively on his or her current campus may be able to dissemble as well in person as on the phone. I have seen committees helped by this kind of campus visit, but I have also seen them misled. It may seem like a foolproof last step, but it is not. And it is extremely disruptive for the candidates. They may have tolerated an open campus interview, but they may balk at the idea of your visiting their campus, particularly if you are visiting more than one candidate. The candidate who is not selected may be very embarrassed in front of colleagues. Considering the hazards for candidates and the limited value for the committee, I recommend against these visits.

Preparing a Committee Recommendation

At the end of the second-round interviews, after campus responses have been gathered, tallied, and summarized, and after all reference checks are complete, including calls to those not listed as references, the committee is ready to prepare its recommendation. Begin by reviewing the charge to the committee so that you are clear about what you have been asked to do—rank-order candidates, present a list of all finalists with strengths and weaknesses, present exactly three candidates or two to four candidates, and so on. The committee should deliberate about the candidates and formulate statements of their strengths and weaknesses. Following an hour or two for this deliberation, the president or the board chair can be asked to join the meeting to discuss the report and ask questions. Or, the committee chair can present the report to the president or board chair at a subsequent meeting.

In a vice presidential search, the president is the appointing officer. Presidents often reserve certain key reference conversations for themselves, such as a call to the president of the finalists' current institutions. The president normally has interviewed the finalists at least once during their second-round campus interviews. And normally, if the president feels there is no one in the pool worthy of appointment, that would have been signaled to the committee earlier. Moving from a committee recommendation to a selection in a vice presidential search should go smoothly.

In a presidential search, the process is more complicated because of the role of the board and the number of people potentially involved. Some boards charge search committees with rank-ordering the candidates, and the board is expected to ratify the committee's choice. In that case, the committee should select the preferred candidate but also rank-order any other finalists so that, if an agreement is not reached with the preferred candidate, the board can turn to the next candidate.

In other cases, the board decides to reserve for itself the selection of the new president, drawing heavily upon committee appraisal of strengths and weaknesses but making its own decision. The search committee presents the board with a short list of candidates, unranked, with strengths and weaknesses, rather than a ranked list or a single preferred candidate. As the board selects a president, a solid base of information should be provided for board review. The committee should give the board the finalists' letters of application and CVs, as well as a summary appraisal of strengths and weaknesses of each finalist. In addition, the committee might provide the written reference reports or a summary of the references, a summary of other background checks that have been done (e.g., verification of educational credentials and employment, Web searches), and results of campus feedback following the second-round interviews. All those receiving the materials or participating in the deliberations must be reminded of the need for confidentiality both during and after the process.

Ideally, some or all board members will have met and interviewed the finalists when they visited the campus during the second-round interviews. If few have been able to do that, an additional visit by the candidates for board interviews may be required; these conversations give board members an opportunity to make their own appraisal of the candidates, but they also give presidential candidates the opportunity to make an appraisal of the board—the president's most important constituency.

The process of selecting the first-choice candidate sometimes moves smoothly and swiftly, and sometimes is protracted and difficult. In some searches, a consensus emerges that is reinforced by repeated conversations with the candidates and by reports from references. The accomplishments of one candidate in particular are impressive and have been well documented, the candidate's colleagues all speak enthusiastically and credibly about his or her work, and everyone who met the candidate comes away delighted and eager to welcome this person and his or her family into the community. While the other candidates may have many strengths, none compares to the preferred candidate, and the board or the president have no doubt.

Considering Extending the Search

Sometimes, the finalist pool contains no one who is so compelling. As the committee reviews the finalists, there may be serious reservations about all of them. Often there is the wish to do some splicing—to combine the administrative talents of one with the fund-raising skills of a second and the demeanor of a third. And very often, the committee, the president or the board in this situation grapple with the question of whether to continue the search in the hope that someone perfect is lurking just around the corner. The challenge is to know when the candidates really are inadequate, and when the candidates are drawn from the top tier of likely candidates for this position, at this institution, in this location, at this time in its development, at this salary. It is always possible that there might be someone better, but it is also possible that you will not find anyone better. If you extend the search, you will lose the good candidates whom you currently have.

The process of extended searching has not only a price in time and effort and campus morale, but also a reputational price, as candidates and others observe the institution's unsuccessful search. The *Chronicle of Higher Education* regularly reports on this kind of situation, so the news of your difficulties can be magnified. There can be no simple answer to the question of whether a search should be extended, but those responsible for making the decision should remember that this is a common dilemma. If you are working with a consultant, he or she may be able to help you speculate about the potential to identify stronger candidates in an extended search by reviewing the extent of recruiting already done and the kinds of responses received from those who declined. If you are working without a consultant, consider what additional recruiting efforts you would make in an extended search and how likely these are to yield a better pool of interested candidates. With or without a consultant, this is the time to consider whether the position should be redefined, the resources enhanced, or the compensation package improved in order to attract a stronger group of candidates in an extended search.

Timing of the Final Steps

It is important to remember as you move into the final stages of the search process that you do not have full control of your candidates. While you are busy judging and selecting them, they are also considering whether they want to accept the position if offered, stay where they are (perhaps with a counteroffer), or accept another offer that they may have received or may hope to receive in the coming days. Candidates may have been asked whether they are in other searches, or what reservations they have about accepting your position if it is offered, but that does not guarantee that they will accept. When you review your finalists and select your favorite, consider whether you would appoint the second-ranked candidate, and even the third-ranked candidate, if the higher-ranked candidates were to disappear at the last minute.

Time is of the essence. The longer the process from second-round interviews to an offer, the greater the risks to the successful completion of the search. In addition to the risks described above, there are the added risks of annoyance and second thoughts. Candidates may begin to feel that your institution is too disorganized or divided to be attractive, or they may suspect that you are negotiating with someone else and that they are seen as second best, or they may reflect and talk with colleagues and family and decide that the offer is not so attractive as they thought during the excitement of the interviews. Plan from the beginning of the search to move swiftly through the final stages. If this means scheduling special board meetings, or a board conference call, or delegating the decision to the executive committee, you should do these things and plan in advance to bring the search to a prompt conclusion.

If you are fortunate enough to have more than one very attractive candidate, and you extend an offer to the top choice, how long will that candidate take to reach a decision? Some searches take a very aggressive approach, asking two or more finalists to commit in advance of the institution's decision that they would accept if offered. Although this may seem like a smart strategy, guaranteeing a swift final step in the process, I find it unattractive. It places candidates in a very difficult position psychologically, and since, as a consultant, it is normally my job to give the bad news to any candidate not selected, I sympathize with those on the receiving end of my unhappy call. Unless all the terms of the offer are on the table before the offer is actually extended, the candidate cannot really know whether the compensation package will be adequate, and the candidate knows that his or her negotiating strength may be limited after agreeing to accept.

As the search proceeds, the committee chair should talk to the strongest candidates to learn about their compensation expectations and to let them know whether or not those expectations fall within the salary range the institution is able to provide. Issues of concern to the candidate should be identified, if not fully resolved—e.g., housing, car, and other perks; employment or an institutional role for the spouse or partner; starting date; staffing for the office; and other critical resource questions. There should be few if any surprises when the offer is extended. Once the board has decided who should receive the offer, the board chair or the consultant should phone the candidate to extend the offer and reach agreement on the terms.

Assuming that you approach the selected candidate with an offer, what happens next? If the candidate's family has already come to see the campus and community and look at housing, and if there has been enough opportunity for the candidate to learn everything that is needed during the previous interviews and visits, perhaps no additional visit will be needed. A fully informed candidate may only need a couple of days to reflect and talk with family members or trusted advisors before calling the board chair back with a decision. But if you have not provided for a family visit and if you have not provided enough information to the candidate, then he or she may well ask for time to come back to campus, have more conversations, and gather more information. This prolongs the process, and it also creates potential problems in relation to the next candidate on your list. Avoid this situation by making sure that the preceding steps in the search process attended to all these things. It is reasonable to ask a candidate to take no more than a week to make a decision. Candidates who want more visits and more information, and who seem to be covering ground already covered, may be moving toward declining your offer. You either need to intensify your recruiting efforts, or press for a decision so you can present an offer to the next candidate in line.

Negotiating a Compensation Package

Part of the final stage of the search is of course negotiating a compensation package. Most institutions do this themselves with assistance from the institution's attorney and the search consultant. The attorney may draft a letter of agreement that stipulates, at a minimum, salary, bonus potential, starting date and length of term, and whether the position carries academic rank or tenure. Other useful contract elements are broad goals and expectations and the procedures for evaluating performance, understandings about termination for cause and termination without cause, whether a residence is provided and with what conditions and provision for payment of costs, provision for moving expenses, provision of a car, memberships in clubs that can be used for entertaining institutional guests, other benefits such as tuition for the candidate's spouse or children, and sabbatical leaves. A complex letter of agreement will likely lead to more extended discussion and is also likely to require review by the candidate's attorney, as well as by the institution's attorney. There are also attorneys who specialize in the employment contracts of college and university presidents and vice presidents, and who may provide detailed compensation information for peer institutions, and who may represent one of the parties or even, in some cases, both parties. Again, you should avoid delays at this stage by drafting the employment contract in advance and discussing key provisions with the candidates who are moving toward a possible offer. Certainly the board or the president should have established a salary range and, if there is an absolute maximum, or if the maximum is lower than might be expected for this position, candidates should be made aware of it long before the final negotiations begin.

Negotiations sometimes go very smoothly. The candidate knows what to expect and is eager to accept. In some public institutions, it is understood that the offer will be made within hours of the final interview and must be accepted on the spot.

But other times, negotiations can go very badly. I have seen candidates insist on compensation packages that the institution is unwilling or unable to provide.

A candidate may judge his or her worth more generously than the institution judges it, expecting to be at the top of the stated range while the board or president determine that a point lower in the range is more appropriate for a first-time president or vice president. Or, the institution may say, "For the right person, we will pay whatever we have to pay," but it emerges during negotiations that the person selected is just not right enough to command the salary requested. There are often equity issues in setting salary, either by comparison with the faculty and staff, or by comparison with other senior officers, and this can make it difficult to raise the new person's salary as high as might otherwise be appropriate. Clearly if there is a strong second-ranked candidate waiting in the wings, it is a lot easier for the institution to hold down its salary offer. I have seen several candidates become difficult or demanding during the negotiation process to the point that the offer is rescinded. Candidates should be aware that sometimes when a generous compensation package is provided that later becomes public, others on campus realize that the president's or vice president's salary is out of line with their salaries and significant dissent can erupt. The board and candidate need to decide how much controversy they wish to incur.

The President's House

In compensation packages for presidents of colleges and universities, there is often a unique element, provided for only one position and in few sectors other than higher education—the president's house. *The American College President* reports that in the 2001 survey, 44 percent of presidents of private institutions had a president's house, as did 25 percent of presidents of public institutions.[3] If a president's house is not provided, many institutions provide a housing allowance.

The president's house has potential to enhance the sense of community through presidential entertaining of faculty, staff, and students, and potential to enhance fund-raising through the ability to entertain donors in the president's house, but it also has great potential to be a source of controversy. If it is located close to the campus, the house has both the advantage and disadvantage of presidential visibility. Presidents like to see students walking by on their way to class or tossing Frisbees on the lawn, but they may be uneasy about walking down the driveway in a bathrobe to pick up the paper each morning. The life of the president and his or her family is very public, and if it is lived in the fishbowl of a campus house, that public quality can become burdensome. Given a choice, I suspect that most presidents would prefer not to have the president's house right on the campus. But usually there is no choice—the house already exists and by tradition the president either does or does not live in it. Changing this tradition will carry its own burdens. It should be made clear to candidates in advance whether the president is required to live in the official president's house, or expected by custom and tradition to live there. Candidates should also talk with their tax and financial advisors about the potential tax consequences of living in an institutionally owned home.

The date when the new president can occupy the house may have to be negotiated. The incoming president will likely be eager to settle into permanent living arrangements as soon as the presidency begins, and at least some redecorating is usually expected before moving in. The outgoing president may be asked to vacate the home before his or her term ends. The outgoing president needs appropriate housing until the presidency ends, and the board should cover the costs of housing, especially if an early departure from the house has been requested in order to accommodate the incoming president.

If the house is owned by the institution, the expenses associated with its upkeep are normally covered, including both routine and major maintenance, cleaning, and care for lawn and gardens. Entertaining expenses associated with college or university business would also normally be covered. Some institutions provide a daily or weekly housekeeper who may also cook meals for the president and his or her family. How all these expenses will be handled should be made clear from the start.

The greatest hazard associated with the president's house surrounds the cost of renovations and furnishings. The installation of a spa, a home theater, a dog-run, an elevator, or a gourmet kitchen at substantial cost can trigger outbursts of anger from those who cannot afford these features in their own homes and resent the use of institutional funds, taxpayer funds, or even the gift of a special donor for what is defined as the personal enjoyment of the president. No matter how valuable these features may be for entertaining donors, or how essential to accommodate the president's infirm parent, there may be considerable resentment that can be explosive. If there are other sources of anger or resentment about decisions made or leadership style or the pace of change initiated by the new president, the expenses associated with the president's house can be a lightning rod, attracting and providing a focus for accumulated anger. Investments in the president's residence should be undertaken mindful of these risks. The board should consider updating or upgrading the house before the new president is selected so that he or she is not saddled with this potential controversy.

Family Issues

Issues associated with the president's family can sometimes be elements in the negotiation, but even if they are not, a shared understanding should be established as the search process concludes. The underlying question is how best to balance the expectations of the institutional community and the expectations of the president and his or her family members. Institutions that have been comfortable with the role of the president's spouse usually want and expect to see it replicated by the successor, whereas institutions that have been uneasy about the heavy involvement of the spouse in institutional matters, or the total absence of the spouse from institutional events, may want to see a change. Institutions that are used to male presidents who have wives may have to rethink their expectations when they appoint a female president who has a husband. Similarly, appointing a single president, or a president with a live-in significant other, or a gay or lesbian president who may or may not openly have a partner, or a lay president with a spouse when all previous presidents have been celibate clergy —all these will require some rethinking of expectations if the institution is used to a husband and wife. The new president should take the lead in shaping these expectations based on personal decisions, but should do this with sufficient knowledge about traditions and expectations to avoid missteps. The board should take responsibility for giving the incoming president a sense of what these expectations are.

Various elements of the family members' lives may have an impact on the presidency. For example, the president's spouse may or may not be employed, and may or may not move from the previous community to the new community at the start of the presidency. Spouses with full-time jobs and spouses who do not move to the new community are likely to be less available to participate in the life of the institution. The new president and the president's family will, again, want to make these decisions about their lifestyle with a full understanding of traditions and expectations, and the institution's expectations may have to be modified in light of the family's preferences. Occasionally when presidencies end early, others observe that "his wife was never really happy here" or "her husband never moved to the community" as sources of trouble.

The spouse who devotes substantial time to supporting the president through hosting, meeting with donors, traveling, and playing an active role in institutional life, may expect to be recognized and in some cases compensated for this contribution. Some presidential spouses request recognition in the form of compensation. Others, concerned that compensation will entail unwanted accountability, prefer only a title. The titles used include, for example, associate to/of the president, assistant to the president, senior adviser to the president and senior councillor for external relations. Many other spousal and partner issues may call for discussion, including authorization to drive state-owned vehicles, payment for travel expenses when the couple travels on institutional business, retirement benefits, and staff support.[4]

Leadership on the issue of the president's spouse or partner has come primarily from the sector organizations—Association of American Universities (AAU) for the major research institutions, American Association of State Colleges and Universities (AASCU) for the regional comprehensive institutions, Council of Independent Colleges (CIC) for the small private colleges, and so on— and prospective presidents should consult with the relevant organization for advice about these issues as ideas and practices evolve. Appendix K provides the guidelines developed by the AAU.

Notifying Other Finalists

It is essential that, as soon as the successful candidate has accepted the institution's offer, all other finalists be called immediately. After months of involvement in the search process, they are likely to be extremely disappointed, and hearing the news from a reporter or a colleague is very bad form and an unnecessary wound. If there is no consultant, the search chair or the board chair should phone the candidate as soon as possible. There are many ways to deliver the news, but most candidates are not ready at this moment for full and candid feedback. Typically they want to take some time first to digest the information, and sometimes they will call back a few days later to see if there is something they can learn. You may want to offer some comments that can ease the candidate's pain, such as "This was a very difficult decision and the board spent several hours in deliberation," "You did a wonderful interview" or "Your references spoke so warmly about you."

Occasionally candidates are litigious, so the person delivering the information should be careful about what he or she says. You do not want to say, for example, "The board decided that we really wanted someone younger," or "Our institution just isn't ready for a woman president." You also do not want to say, "You really were the first choice of the faculty, but in the end the board decided we needed to hire someone with more strength in fund-raising." Imagine that anything you say about the views of particular constituencies can quickly enter the electronic grapevine and seriously undermine the effectiveness or confidence of the person who did get the job. The greatest hazards in conversations with finalists who were not selected lies in saying too much; without knowing how the candidate might respond, you should say less rather than more. A safe comment is, "You would have brought a great deal to this presidency, and were well received, but in the end we decided that the other candidate was a better fit for our needs at this time."

Just as a representative of the search committee notified candidates that their application materials were received, all candidates should be notified at the end of the search that an appointment has been made. Candidates other than finalists can be notified by mail or e-mail, as soon as possible after the selection.

Announcing the Appointment

Before the public announcement, consider who needs to receive a personal phone call from the board chair or president—e.g., emeritus trustees or major donors, key community leaders, and certainly the search committee. The candidate will also need some time to make personal calls before the announcement is public.

Once those calls are completed, a press release can be distributed externally, and an e-mail message or Web posting can be used internally to the institution. Announcement of the appointment of a president or vice president should be coordinated between the appointing institution and the candidate's current institution.

NOTES

1. Malcolm Gladwell. *Blink: The Power of Thinking without Thinking* (New York: Little, Brown and Company, 2005), 14, 252.

2. Elaine D. Pulakos and Neal Schmitt. "Experience-based and Situational Interview Questions: Studies of Validity," *Personnel Psychology* 48 (1995): 300.

3. Melanie Corrigan, *The American College President* (Washington, DC: American Council on Education, 2002), 45.

4. Also see Julianne Basinger, "A Paycheck for Presidents' Spouses?" *Chronicle of Higher Education*, Sept. 22, 2000; and Raymond D. Cotton, "Paying the President's Spouse," *Chronicle of Higher Education*, May 23, 2003.

CHAPTER 15

Transition to New Leadership

As the search concludes with the appointment of a new president or vice president, the transition has already begun. In a sense, the transition began when the previous incumbent announced his or her departure, and the transition extends through any interim appointment, through the search, through the arrival of the new person as a full-time member of the administration, and finally through the period of institutional adjustment to new leadership. When the appointment begins, it may have been two years since the campus had a full leadership team in place.[1]

PREPARING THE CAMPUS FOR NEW LEADERSHIP

The appointing officer—the board chair in the case of presidential appointments, and the president in the case of vice presidential appointments—should take the lead in presenting the new member of the institution's leadership team. It is this person's voice that speaks directly at public events, and indirectly through press releases and memos to the campus. Normally these messages contain several important elements, such as:

- We are pleased and proud that such a distinguished person is taking on this new responsibility; there will be public events scheduled for the community and especially for those who have not yet had an opportunity to meet him or her.
- We celebrate the excellent work and dedication of the previous person in the position.
- We deeply appreciate the hard work of all those who participated in the search process.
- We are grateful for all those who played important leadership roles since the previous person left the position.
- We anticipate that the new person will join us for certain periods before taking office full-time (e.g., one week out of each month for the next three months, or one day of each week, or for special events).

- A transition team has been established, including, for example, board representatives, some or all of the senior officers, the public relations officer, faculty, staff, and student leadership, and some members of the search committee. In the case of a presidential appointment, the transition team would also include some of those who will have responsibility for preparing for inaugural events.

If there is controversy surrounding the appointment, the appointing officer should anticipate and consider addressing it—but sometimes there may be nothing to be said, or engaging in debate may only exacerbate the dissatisfaction.

Internal Candidates Who Were Not Selected

Because of a concern that internal candidates who were not selected might attract dissent, internal candidates sometimes are encouraged to leave, and sometimes they themselves feel that leaving is the only option. But in other situations, the newly appointed person may identify a valued role for the internal candidate. An attractive external candidate who was not appointed can also be the focus of dissent. That person may be perceived as the first choice of the faculty or of the administration. It is important for the board or the president to anticipate these kinds of concerns so that they are not surprised or undone by conflict that may emerge. Ideally, one hopes that the new person arrives and is so compelling and effective that he or she quickly wins the support of all constituencies and individuals—including the internal candidate and his or her supporters, who can easily see the strengths that led to the selection. Ideally, the internal candidate is eager to work for and learn from this new colleague. Needless to say, it is not always this simple!

THE ROLE OF THE SEARCH COMMITTEE

The search committee does not necessarily play an active role during the transition. In fact, the greatest risk is that committee members will be too active, and too vocal, potentially breaching the confidentiality that should not cease at the conclusion of the search. The temptation to let one's guard down now that the search is concluded is very great. Committee members have inside stories to share—the back-channel references that torpedoed a leading candidate, the arguments in search committee meetings, divisions in the committee about what the most important selection criteria should be, who was the favorite candidate of each constituency, etc. Often there is a celebratory event at the end of the search; it should provide another occasion to remind committee members of their commitment to keep permanently confidential everything that occurred during the search.

PREPARING FOR NEW LEADERSHIP

The goal of the search is to select the best new leadership for the institution. Board members may anticipate that the new president will slip smoothly into the new role and that the board can relax now that its most important decision has been well made. For experienced presidents, this is relatively but not completely true; even an experienced president will need support in understanding this institution's culture and traditions, and in building relationships with community leaders, major donors, and the full board of trustees, including emeritus members. And first-time presidents, as well prepared as they may be, will need particular support. Many new presidents find it very valuable to attend one of the programs developed for new presidents; Appendix A includes a list of these programs. The same things apply to new vice presidents.

The conclusion of the search is clearly, as they say at commencement, both an end and a beginning. A major question has been resolved—who will be the new president or vice president? But many other questions have barely been asked, and have surely not been answered yet. Will the fit be as good as everyone hopes? Will the new person define a new institutional direction and new priorities? Will he or she clean house or move forward with the current leadership team? Will the necessary resources be assembled to carry out the mission and achieve the institutional aspirations? If the search has been done well, all these questions will have been explored in a preliminary way, and all those involved will be pleased to see that the search has established a strong foundation for successful new leadership.

NOTES

1. For information about the broad range of transition issues that occur during this long period, see essays in James Martin, James E. Samels & Associates, *Presidential Transition in Higher Education: Managing Leadership Change* (Baltimore MD: The Johns Hopkins University Press, 2004).

Appendix A:
Professional Development Programs

PROGRAMS OF THE AMERICAN ASSOCIATION OF
STATE COLLEGES AND UNIVERSITIES (AASCU)

- *Millennium Leadership Initiative (MLI)*: The MLI, a focused leadership development program designed to strengthen the preparation and eligibility of persons who are traditionally underrepresented in the roles of president or chancellor, prepares the next generation of campus leaders. Participants include senior-level administrators (dean level or above), particularly individuals from underrepresented populations, who wish to advance in their careers. The program is a four-day institute followed by a yearlong mentoring component. For additional information, see http:/www.aascu.org/mli/default.htm.

- *New Presidents Academy:* This intensive four-day program addresses the challenges facing state college and university presidents during their first 500 days in office. The program, led by experienced and successful presidents, focuses on such topics as team building, advocacy, financial management, fund-raising, and planning one's entry strategy. Participants include presidents and chancellors at AASCU member campuses who have taken office within the past two years. For additional information, contact Chris Bitting at bittingc@aascu.org.

- *Seeking The Presidency:* This is a special free three-hour seminar offered to participants annually in both the winter and summer Academic Affairs meetings of AASCU, exploring both broad issues (the nature of the presidency, readiness for the job, long term preparation, etc.) and specific search issues (designing a resume, writing a letter of application, interviewing, role of search consultants, etc.). Participants are chief academic officers at AASCU institutions. For additional information, contact George Mehaffy at mehaffyg@aascu.org.

PROGRAMS OF THE
AMERICAN COUNCIL ON EDUCATION (ACE)

- *ACE Fellows Program:* This program identifies and prepares senior faculty and administrators to become skilled in the leadership of institutional change. It provides on-the-job experience as well as a didactic component. Participation is by application. For additional information, contact leadership_programs@ace.nche.edu.

- *Advancing to the Presidency:* This workshop for chief academic officers and other vice presidents provides an opportunity for those seeking a presidency within the next year or two to gain valuable insight into the process of becoming a campus CEO. The two-day workshop focuses on presidential leadership, the CEO search process, contract negotiation, and successful transitions into the presidency. The highly interactive program includes candid conversations with search firm executives, coaching by current presidents from diverse institutions, feedback from mock interviews, and critiques of cover letters and CV/resume packages. For additional information, contact the Center for Effective Leadership at (202) 939-9728, or leadership_programs@ace.nche.edu.

- *Institute for New Chief Academic Officers:* This institute is designed for CAOs in their first three years on the job, providing practical executive leadership development through a yearlong series of three meetings. The institute enables participants to explore a broad range of leadership issues, including making difficult strategic and financial decisions, managing academic personnel, setting and evaluating institutional and personal agendas, leading change (and stability), and working with key internal and external constituencies. For additional information, contact the Center for Effective Leadership at (202) 939-9728, or leadership_programs@ace. nche.edu.

- *National Leadership Forums for the Advancement of Women Leaders:* Each forum brings together presidents to work with women who are ready to move into senior administrative positions or presidencies. The three-day event, limited to 25 participants, offers discussions of issues and challenges surrounding leadership in the academy and introduces participants to a number of search consultants who prepare them to engage in the search process. For additional information, contact leadership_programs@ace.nche.edu.

- *Regional Leadership Forums:* The Office of Women in Higher Education offers these forums for emerging and mid-level women academic administrators who are ready to move into deanships and vice presidencies. The three-day events offer discussion of issues and challenges surrounding leadership in the academy, especially strategic planning, resource allocation, and fund-raising. The participants are introduced to a number of search consultants who prepare them to engage in the search process. For additional information, contact leadership_programs@ace.nche.edu.

- *Summits for Women Presidents* and *Summits for Presidents of Color:* These summits are designed to explore the challenges and opportunities of the presidency for these groups, provide direct support and service to sitting presidents, establish a peer network, and foster collaborations among presidents and with association leaders, government officials, and higher-education scholars and consultants. For additional information, contact leadership_programs@ace.nche.edu.

PROGRAMS OF THE
COUNCIL OF INDEPENDENT COLLEGES (CIC)

- *New Presidents Program:* This program offers opportunities for new presidents and their spouses to meet and exchange ideas with other newcomers and learn the ins and outs of a wide range of presidential issues. The presenters are experienced presidents, many of them alumni of the program. The New Presidents Program is held on January 3 and 4 each year, immediately preceding CIC's Presidents Institute (January 4–7). For additional information, see http:/www.cic.edu/conferences_ events/presidents/2007newpres.asp.

- *Presidential Vocation and Institutional Mission:* This seminar-based program is designed to assist current and prospective presidents in affirming their own sense of vocation, in the context of the missions of the institutions they lead and might lead in the future. There are two seminars—one for presidents and their spouses, and the other for prospective presidents and their spouses. Each of the seminars consists of a two-day meeting in the summer, followed by a two-day follow-up meeting in the winter. For additional information, see http:/www.cic.edu/projects_services/ grants/vocation_mission.asp.

- *Workshop for Chief Academic Officers in Their Third or Fourth Year of Service:* This half-day workshop is designed for chief academic officers in their third or fourth year of service who may be ready to move into a new stage of leadership with a focus on truly leading, rather than managing, the institution. It is offered each year during CIC's Institute for Chief Academic Officers, which is always held over the first full weekend in November. For additional information, see http:/www.cic.edu/ conferences_events/caos/2006.asp#workshops.

- *Workshop for New Chief Academic Officers:* This daylong workshop for new chief academic officers and their spouses is designed to meet the needs of those in their first year of office and is led by experienced colleagues. It is offered each year, on the day prior to the beginning of CIC's Institute for Chief Academic Officers, which is always held over the first full weekend in November. For additional information, see http:/www.cic.edu/conferences_events/caos/2006.asp#newcao&caomentor.

PROGRAMS OF THE
HARVARD INSTITUTES FOR HIGHER EDUCATION

- *Harvard Seminar for New Presidents (HSNP):* HSNP provides newly appointed presidents with a practical and conceptual orientation to the presidency. Participants are first-time presidents who have been appointed but not yet assumed office or who are in the first year of their tenure as president. Acting or interim presidents are not eligible. The program meets for six days, typically in mid-to-late July. For additional information, see http:/www.gse.harvard.edu/ppe.

- *Institute for Educational Management (IEM):* IEM provides an opportunity for senior-level administrators to examine critical challenges facing higher education by focusing on the qualities necessary for effective leadership, especially during times of major institutional change. Participants include members of the president's cabinet (presidents, provosts, vice presidents, and other members of the chief executive's senior leadership team). The program is 12 days, typically in late July/early August. For additional information, see http:/www.gse.harvard.edu/ppe.

- *Institute for Management and Leadership in Education (MLE):* MLE prepares participants to lead organizational change by providing information and insights necessary to help institutions respond to a rapidly shifting competitive environment. The program addresses two central questions: How well positioned is my organization to

meet current and future challenges? How effective is my own leadership? Participants include experienced senior-level administrators (vice presidents and deans)
who are responsible for thinking strategically about their institutions' change agendas. The program is 12 days, typically in late June. For additional information, see
http:/www.gse.harvard.edu/ppe.

- *Management Development Program (MDP):* MDP is designed to provide new perspectives and practical insights for college and university administrators who must
  "manage from the middle" by providing a more sophisticated understanding of the
  functioning of different institutional units and how they should best work together
  to support broader institutional goals. Participants include administrators in the
  early years of their professional careers (vice presidents, deans, directors, and department heads). The program is 12 days, typically in late June. For additional information, see http:/www.gse.harvard.edu/ppe.

Appendix B: Reference Lists

For each person listed as a reference, provide the full name and title; e-mail address; and home, work, and cell telephone numbers, if the reference is willing to receive calls at those numbers. For each reference, provide a brief explanation of the context in which he or she knows you (e.g., supervisor, peer, chair of a committee on which you served, or colleague in a professional association).

Reference lists should be assembled with the following considerations in mind:

- *360 degrees:* Submit a list that yields a 360-degree profile, including at least one person to whom you have reported (preferably currently), a person who has reported to you, and someone at the same level as you within your institution.

- *Focus on the position you are applying for:* Consider the nature of the position and include references who can describe your ability to carry out its responsibilities. This is an especially important consideration for candidates who hold a different type of position. For example, if you are a vice president who is a candidate for a presidency, identify references who can comment on presidential responsibilities such as the ability to raise funds, work with the board, work with legislators, etc.

- *Include members of key constituencies:* This will depend on the position for which you are a candidate. For example, candidates for president should include faculty, staff, administrators, students, alumni, donors, trustees, and community members. Candidates for vice president should include experienced vice presidents who can attest to your readiness to move to that level.

- *Use primarily references who know you well:* Focus on references who know you well and can talk about working with you on a daily basis. Candidates may list one or two names of people with whom they worked at annual conferences and other off-campus activities, but these should be used sparingly.

- *Include references from several different institutions:* Candidates who have been at the same institution for a very long time should use references from other institutions to help demonstrate their awareness of issues and solutions at other institutions and nationally.

- *Include diverse colleagues:* The reference list should include men, women, and people of varied racial and ethnic backgrounds.

- *Be cautious about listing mentors and friends:* Individuals who are your mentors and friends may lack credibility as references.

- *Be cautious about listing too many individuals at lower levels of the organization:* Listing one or two individuals at lower levels reflects an awareness that you must be effective in working in all directions. Listing too many staff at lower levels suggests that you do not have support among senior leaders who can comment on your fitness to serve at the senior level.

- *List counterparts of committee members:* Committee members may wish to call peers as references. For example, a dean on the committee might call a dean for a reference, or the president of the student government organization might call his or her counterpart. Considering the typical search committee composition, candidates should therefore consider including trustees, administrators, faculty members, students, and members of the external community on the list of references.

Appendix C:
Interview Guide

Search committees should select questions that are linked to the professional qualifications and personal characteristics that they are looking for, and should shape the questions to reflect the specifics of the institution. The following questions are offered as examples. Comments are offered on some questions to assist committees in thinking about the approach they wish to take. Many of the questions are far too long to be asked as written here; committees can decide how to focus their questions. Questions framed here for presidential searches can easily be reframed for vice presidential searches.

INTERVIEW GUIDELINES FOR THE SEARCH CHAIR

- Begin with introductions so that candidates know to whom they are speaking. They should have been given a list of names and titles before coming to the interview, and introductions will allow them to link names and faces. Each committee member should have a table-tent with his or her name.

- Remember that you are recruiting as well as screening. Committee members should adopt a conversational tone rather than appearing to be grilling candidates in an effort to uncover their flaws.

- The committee should use a broadly standardized set of questions. However, it is not a script and can be modified if necessary. Ask few enough questions to leave time for follow-up questions.

- The chair usually asks the first question, and subsequent questions should be asked by other members of the committee. If possible, every committee member should ask at least one question.

- If you notice that a candidate is not using examples, the chair should encourage him or her to do so.

- The last 10 minutes of each interview should be reserved for candidates to ask their questions.

SAMPLE QUESTIONS

1. INTRODUCTION: *It is a good idea to begin with a "softball" question that essentially gives candidates the opportunity to tell you about themselves. There are many*

ways to frame this question. The response serves to remind committee members about the highlights of the candidates' experience, helps everyone to settle down and focus on the upcoming conversation, and is broad enough to allow candidates to make the remarks that they may have prepared (whether or not they were requested to do so).

The response to this question will give you some indication of whether the candidate is likely to go on at great or even excessive length in his or her responses. Some candidates can spend half the interview on this question. If the candidate goes on too long, the chair may want to mention before the next question is asked that there are eight or nine questions and the candidate should be mindful of time constraints.

We have reviewed your materials and are eager to learn more about you. Would you begin by telling us what special strengths and experiences you bring to the position of _____? Are there any areas in which you think your background is less strong?

2. *VISION: Committee members often want to ask candidates what their vision is for this institution. I recommend against asking the question in this way; see Chapter 14 for discussion of this topic. Alternative approaches might include the following:*

   - For presidential candidates: Everything that we do here at _____ University should be done in the context of an overall vision, as articulated by the president. What experience have you had with articulating a vision and engaging others in its implementation? What might be your vision for _____ University?

   - For vice presidential candidates: What experience have you had in articulating a vision for your area of responsibility, within the context of the broad vision set by the president? What might be your vision for your area of responsibility at _____ University?

3. *STRATEGIC PLANNING:* We have a strong commitment to a very active strategic planning process, and the president is responsible for leading that process, in close collaboration with the board. Can you describe your experience with leading a strategic planning process, with implementing a plan, and with using the plan as a decision-making tool?

4. *ADMINISTRATIVE EXPERIENCE:* A fundamental responsibility of the president is to run the university, managing people and resources effectively. Would you tell us about the management experience you have had that is most similar to this, and describe the areas of your greatest administrative strength and your greatest administrative challenge relative to our presidency?

5. *MANAGEMENT:* Managing our complex structure and our patterns of growth [or decline] will require a lot of skill. Can you tell us about the most complex management situation you have faced and give us some examples that show how you created a plan, communicated with various audiences, allocated and reallocated resources, and made the difficult decisions? We would appreciate it if you could be specific in showing your role in the situation you describe.

6. *DECISION MAKING*: How do you go about making complex decisions, such as the allocation of scarce resources, the response to a scandal within a winning athletic team, the continuation or discontinuance of an academic program, or the termination of a popular faculty member? Choose an example and describe how you balanced your own judgment and the input of others, and how you dealt with those who opposed the decision you made. If you had it to do over again, would you make the same or a different decision?

7. *FINANCIAL MANAGEMENT*: We have a complex financial structure. While the vice president for finance naturally handles the detailed management of resources and proposes financial strategy, the overall strategy must ultimately be approved by the president. Would you tell us about the most complex financial affairs you have managed, describe a success in that arena, and also tell us about an unfortunate experience or decision you have made?

8. *COMMUNICATION ABOUT FINANCIAL ISSUES*: One of the CFO's responsibilities is to communicate about financial issues—to the faculty, the administration, and the board of trustees. Thinking about the different needs of each of these audiences, what experience have you had communicating with these groups? What is your inclination regarding sharing complex financial information and bad news?

9. *LEADERSHIP FOR GROWTH OR DECLINE: Here is a series of alternative questions, which should be shaped to reflect the specifics of your institution.*

   - We are a growing campus with many critical decisions ahead as to how and where and how quickly we should grow. What experience have you had working in this kind of situation? Did you learn any lessons that would be helpful to you if you were appointed?

   - As you know, we have been experiencing severe enrollment decline with accompanying loss of resources. What experience have you had working in this kind of situation? Did you learn any lessons that would be helpful to you if you were appointed?

   - We have had severe budget cuts in spite of our enrollment growth. What experience have you had working in this kind of situation? Did you learn any lessons that would be helpful to you if you were appointed?

10. *COMMITMENT TO SERVING STUDENTS*: What kinds of relations have you had with students in your administrative positions? What do you think is the role of the president in strengthening the student experience? Do you have any experience with efforts to link the academic program with out-of-classroom programs?

11. *BUILDING A LEADERSHIP TEAM*: The person we appoint will be a "leader of leaders"—selecting a leadership team and supporting their professional development and effectiveness, both individually and collectively. Would you

describe how you have selected, developed, and evaluated the performance of those who have reported to you?

12. *ADVOCACY AND TEAMWORK:* Executives are always balancing advocacy for their own area against supporting broader institutional needs. How have you handled these competing demands in your previous roles? What do you expect of those reporting to you in terms of balancing advocacy and teamwork?

13. *WORKING WITH DIRECT REPORTS:* The vice presidents are actively involved in leading and managing their areas of responsibility. Thinking of those who have reported to you in previous positions, can you describe for us how you find a balance between micromanaging on the one hand, and standing too far back on the other hand?

14. *FUND-RAISING:* The president will have substantial responsibility for fund-raising. Can you tell us about your experience with fund-raising, and the successes you have had? What is the most satisfying element of this responsibility, and what is the most onerous? How would you feel about devoting a great deal of time to generating resources?

15. *COMMUNITY VISIBILITY:* We have been striving to build the visibility of our institution, with many other colleges and universities competing for attention. What experience do you have in building institutional visibility? Would you bring particular skills or ideas to this responsibility?

16. *BOARD RELATIONS:* Our board is well informed and active in institutional leadership. What is your board-relations experience? How do you build consensus within the board for difficult actions? An example would be helpful.

17. *SYSTEM RELATIONS:* Institutions in our state system are typically active partners as well as competitors for resources. Can you describe how you have managed this kind of relationship in your previous responsibilities?

18. *STATE SUPPORT:* Our institution, like virtually every other state university, is state assisted rather than state supported, and we are facing a substantial decline in state allocations. What experience have you had in lobbying at the state level to the state system or board, or to the legislature, for increased funds?

19. *CHURCH-RELATED ISSUES:* Our mission and identity are shaped in part by our affiliation with a religious denomination. Can you tell us what you think it is that makes a university [Catholic, Presbyterian, Lutheran, Jewish, etc.]? What experience have you had in the leadership of a religiously affiliated institution, and how would you approach that responsibility if you were appointed? What would you bring to the role, and in what ways might it be especially challenging for you?

20. ACADEMIC EXCELLENCE: *The following series of items is too complex to be part of a single question. Committee members might separate them so that the candidate has the opportunity to respond to one at a time. Or, you might focus only on certain of the items in the preliminary interview, leaving others for the more detailed discussions in the second-round interview.*

   • Maintaining and enhancing the quality of our people and programs is our highest priority. Can you tell us about your experience with this kind of responsibility?

   • What is your general approach to enhancing quality? For example, do you identify and support particular areas of excellence, or have you sought the highest quality in all areas?

   • Have you been able to generate new resources from outside your institution that have contributed to enhancing quality?

   • How have you dealt with the financial costs of quality? We're interested in your experience with resource allocation and reallocation in support of enhancing quality, and the strategies you have found most effective, both financially and administratively.

   • What have you found to be the greatest barrier to achieving and maintaining excellence?

21. EXPECTATIONS FOR FACULTY:

   • Over the last 10 years, expectations for faculty have shifted. Scholarly productivity has become increasingly important. Have you been involved in this kind of shift in expectations and the controversy that it can engender? What role did you play and how effectively did you navigate the situation?

   • Over the last 10 years, expectations for faculty have shifted. We are increasingly focused on the quality of teaching. Have you been involved in this kind of shift in expectations and controversy that it can engender? What role did you play and how effectively did you navigate the situation?

22. COLLECTIVE BARGAINING: Our faculty have collective bargaining. What experience have you had working with faculty unions? What do you see as the advantages and disadvantages of collective bargaining?

23. DIVERSITY: Enhancing diversity is a high priority for our institution. Would you tell us about your efforts to diversify in all sectors of your institution—faculty, staff, students, and the board? What strategies have you found most effective?

24. COMMUNICATION: In an institution of our size and complexity, it will always be a challenge to communicate fully with all members of the university community, but failures of communication can derail even the best projects. Can you describe a situation in which you believe your communication efforts made

the difference between success and failure, and a situation in which you wish you had communicated more effectively or more fully?

25. *PERSONAL QUALITIES:* If we asked your peers to tell us about you, what would they say? What would your supervisor say? What about the people who report to you?

26. *INTELLECTUAL LIFE:* Can you tell us about how you define your academic contributions as a teacher and a scholar? How have you been able to sustain your intellectual life and your teaching and research commitments while serving as an administrator?

27. *PERSONAL SITUATION:* What career path do you see for yourself, and how would this position fit into that? Is there anything of significance about your personal or professional situation that we have not yet given you an opportunity to tell us about?

28. *AREAS OF CONCERN:* Are there any areas of concern in your professional or personal life that we should be aware of, or that might be an embarrassment for our institution if you were appointed?

29. *INTEGRITY:* A principal consideration in this search is to be certain that the person selected is a person of uncompromising integrity. Can you give us an example in your career when you were faced with a difficult decision and your actions were guided by principles of honesty and integrity?

30. *PROFESSIONAL CHALLENGE:* What has been the greatest challenge in your administrative career, and how did you address it?

Appendix D:
Items to Consider When
Reviewing an Offer

The following items will not all be included in a formal agreement. But these items should be discussed either during the search process or during the final preappointment conversations.

Compensation package

- Salary, and provision for salary adjustment
- Tenure, rank, and faculty status
- Length of appointment
- Bonus potential; how it will be evaluated and by whom
- Deferred compensation
- Special compensation associated with length of service
- Housing: If a house is provided, clarify responsibility for various expenses (e.g., major maintenance, redecoration and furnishing, remodeling, routine maintenance, utilities, phone, Internet connection, and homeowner's insurance). If a house is not provided, alternatives include a housing allowance, mortgage supplement, shared purchase, and forgivable loan. Expectations for use of the house for personal and for institutional purposes should be clarified. Clarify who is permitted to live in the house.
- Insurance for the employee and family members
- Retirement contributions
- Tuition for spouse and children at the institution, and at other institutions, for undergraduate or graduate programs
- Tuition for children in K–12 independent schools
- Club memberships
- Automobile and associated expenses, including gas, maintenance, insurance; frequency of car replacement.
- Vacations and other leaves
- Potential for sabbatical leaves

Provisions for evaluation and for separation

- Process for establishing annual goals and evaluating accomplishments: who will be involved, timetable for evaluations, compensation, and other items that may be contingent on accomplishment of goals
- Separation agreements that define separation for cause and without cause; amount of notice to be given before leaving
- Compensation to be provided in the event of separation for cause and without cause

Institutional resources

- Staffing for the president's office
- Authority to appoint and terminate senior staff
- Expectations for board members' philanthropic contributions

Spouse/partner expectations (*See also* Appendix K)

- Potential for spouse or partner to be employed within the institution
- Expectations regarding outside employment
- Expectations regarding travel and entertaining, including responsibility for costs
- Expectations regarding campus activities such as committees
- Availability of staff support for the spouse or partner's institutional work
- Recognition of the spouse or partner's role through title or compensation, including benefits such as retirement accounts

Appendix E:
Search Committee Code of Ethics

A SEARCH COMMITTEE CODE OF ETHICS

Search committees should consider adopting a code of conduct to ensure impartial, ethical, and respectful treatment of candidates, and also to ensure that a decision is reached based on the most complete and accurate information. The following might be a model for such a code.

As members of this search committee, we accept our responsibility to protect the integrity of every prospect and candidate. Accordingly, each of us pledges to adhere to these principles:

1. I acknowledge that only the Chairperson is authorized to speak to the media on behalf of the institution.

2. I certify that I am personally not a candidate for the position.

3. I subscribe to the principle that any appearance of real or potential conflict of interest in the relationship between me and a prospect or candidate should be avoided and that its occurrence will be disclosed promptly to the committee.

4. I pledge to keep as my primary focus the need of the institution to attract a new hire within a timetable that gives it a competitive advantage.

5. I will follow the principles below for the management of information about the work of the committee. This work includes what is developed and received about prospects, candidates, and their employing institutions. I understand this effort is necessary to attract excellent finalists, to avoid putting their current positions in jeopardy, and to maintain my institution's professional image. Specifically, I will adhere to the following code of responsibility, accuracy, and integrity:

    • I pledge to respect the absolute confidentiality of all prospects and candidates. I will not reveal the name of or any information about any prospects or candidates before or after the committee completes its work.

    • I will adhere to the highest standards of ethical and professional conduct.

- I will be fair, accurate, honest, responsible, and decent in my management of information.

- I will avoid practices that would conflict with my ability to be fair and unbiased.

- I will develop my independent opinions prior to group discussions.

- I will guard against inaccuracies, carelessness, bias, and distortion made through either emphasis or omission of information.

- I will admit any misrepresentation of information and correct it promptly and prominently.

- I will strive for impartial treatment of issues and dispassionate handling of controversial subjects. I understand that prospects and candidates who have held executive jobs and made difficult decisions have not necessarily been in positions to win popularity contests.

- I will not permit personal interests to distort or misrepresent the facts.

- I will give reports on candidates to the Chair of the Search Committee for determining their accuracy before the Chair shares the information with others. Reports should be confirmed by three on-the-record sources.

- I understand that no code of ethics can prejudge every situation.

- I will use common sense and good judgment in applying ethical principles to search work.

- I consider the content and intent of this statement to be a matter of personal responsibility.

The concept and several of the principles in this model code of conduct were initiated by the search committee chaired by Frances Hesselbein for the search of the president of Independent Sector. Principles were also borrowed and adapted from the APME (Associated Press Managing Editors) Code of Ethics for Newspapers and their Staff.

Authors: Jan Greenwood, Greenwood & Associates, Inc.
Marlene Ross, director, ACE Fellows Program,
American Council on Education

Source: Educational Record, *Summer 1996.*

Appendix F:
Search Schedule

This scheduling worksheet can be used at the first meeting of the search committee to establish the schedule for the search. The approximate time periods shown under "Date and Time" should be replaced with actual dates and times, and specific locations should be established. The worksheet can be revised periodically as the search proceeds.

SCHEDULING WORKSHEET
Revised on _____

Date and Time	Location	Purpose
August	Campus	• First meeting of the Search Committee with consultant (if a consultant is being used) • Committee and consultant meet with senior administrators andconstituent groups
September	Campus	• Committee meets to finalize text of position specifications • Advertising and recruiting begin
October and November		• Recruiting
Early December	Campus	• Committee reviews candidate files and selects 10–12 for preliminary interviews • Interview questions drafted and finalized
Early January	Airport vicinity hotel	• Committee holds preliminary interviews with 10–12 candidates • Approximately six candidates selected for reference review
Late January		• Reference calls and background checks
Early February	Campus	• Committee reviews reference reports and selects approximately three candidates for second-round interviews

Late February	Campus or off-campus— to be decided	• Second-round interviews
Early March	Campus	• Committee reviews feedback from interviews and prepares recommendations
Mid-March	Campus	• Special meeting of the board of trustees to select preferred presidential candidate; or, president selects preferred vice presidential candidate

Key dates:
  Fall break: _____
  Winter break: _____
  Spring break: _____

  Candidate target response date: _____

Appendix G:
Reviewing Applications

Candidate application materials can be voluminous, and search committee members need strategies for reviewing them that are both appropriate and efficient. Readers will differ in their reading strategies, and different members of the committee bring different levels of knowledge. Some will be more familiar with academic issues, some with student issues, some with external-relations issues, and so on. Although one member of a committee may feel unable to evaluate a candidate in a particular area of activity, another member of the committee may bring expertise in that area. Many important matters will have to be validated through conversations and interviews and through reference checks—the application materials are only the beginning.

The items listed below are a series of filters. For each file you read, consider whether the candidate "passes" your review on Step 1 below. If so, move on to Step 2, Step 3, and so on. If the candidate does not pass your review on Step 1, rate the file accordingly and put it aside. This is intended to save some time reviewing weaker candidates, and it allows you to spend more time on detailed reviews of the stronger candidates. But if you believe that a candidate shows strengths in spite of low ratings on any of these items, you should feel free to rate the candidate highly and then to discuss this with the committee. Make notes that remind you later of why you made each rating.

The items listed below should be adapted to your institutional circumstances. For example, if academic credibility is a higher priority than fund-raising experience, you may want to weight the items below accordingly.

Step 1: Review the career path (usually on the first or second page of the CV).

- Is there enough senior management experience (e.g., several years as a vice president or dean of a large school)?

- Watch for patterns of repeated rapid job changes (such as a series of positions *at different institutions* lasting no more than two years each). Watch for candidates who have stepped down from their positions and are not currently employed. Both of these call for more information.

- Look for breadth of experience (e.g., positions that require attention to a broad range of institution-wide issues rather than only a focused set of issues within a small segment of the institution).

Step 2: Consider credentials.

- Look for credentials that suggest academic credibility in the context of standards and expectations of this institution and position (including doctoral degree, experience as a faculty member, and publications/presentations/grants). If this is a "nontraditional" candidate who comes from outside higher education, look for evidence that he or she has an affinity for the academic world (e.g., teaching experience, service as a university trustee). Some search committees will want to consider whether a candidate is a graduate of the institution.

- Make some preliminary qualitative evaluations (e.g., the quality of the institution from which the candidate's degrees were earned; the location of publications—major journals vs. newsletters; the type of publication—books, articles, book reviews).

- Consider institutional quality. Although there are very talented and capable prospective presidents and vice presidents in institutions of all types, many search committees will be more comfortable with candidates who have worked at or attended institutions of similar stature.

- Special note to faculty members: Keep in mind the difference between evaluating candidates for faculty positions (or even faculty-based positions like dean) and candidates for presidencies or vice presidencies. Success in areas expected of faculty does not necessarily lead to success in administrative roles, and vice versa.

Step 3: Evaluate experiences and accomplishments. Look for information about particular experiences that the search committee has defined as important (see the Rating Sheet in Appendix H for a summary). This will probably be in the candidate's cover letter. If you believe that the best predictor of future success is past performance, look for evidence of that performance—not just unsupported assertions.

- Look for both ideas and the ability to implement. Candidates should have familiarity with both broad conceptual issues (e.g., mission and vision) and operational issues (e.g., managing the budget, revising the curriculum)—depending on what the search has defined as important.

- Seek evidence of leadership. In what ways has the candidate made a significant contribution to shaping the direction or character of an institution or one of its major divisions?

- Consider affinity for your institutional mission and the ability to convey it effectively to others.

- Look for a fit between the candidate's current or former institutions and your institution in terms of type (public or private), approximate size, religious affiliation or values orientation, category (research, doctoral, comprehensive, baccalaureate), and perhaps region or location (rural, suburban, or urban). Each reader will need to decide how important these factors are. Candidates do not have to come from institutions that are precisely like this one, but some general similarity is usually viewed as helpful.

- Look for fund-raising experience. Especially for presidential candidates who are vice presidents for academic affairs, finance or student affairs, there may be no evidence of or experience with fund-raising; this is rarely part of those positions. You will need to decide whether other experiences can substitute for fund-raising as you evaluate the candidate's file and interview.

Step 4: Read the cover letter and look for some of the subtler characteristics. Remember that narrative statements are perceived very subjectively. Reasonable people will disagree about interpretations. Be cautious about putting excessive weight on the cover letter in your evaluation.

- Note basic items such as articulateness and accuracy (spelling, punctuation, consistency, other details)
- Look for reflections of management style, such as inclusiveness, openness in sharing information, and awareness of all segments of the institution
- Look for statements that lead you to believe that this candidate would share the values of this institution

Appendix H:
Candidate Rating Sheet

This rating sheet is designed to assist committee members in organizing their appraisal of the candidates. It reflects the qualifications and characteristics that the committee agreed to look for in candidates. After reading each candidate file, give it an overall rating of A (strong), B (moderate), or C (weak).

Not all items can be evaluated from reading candidate files, so keep this rating sheet and use it as the committee gathers additional information about candidates through interviews and reference checks.

The ideal candidate will have the following professional qualifications and personal characteristics:

Vision and mission: Ability to formulate, articulate, and implement a vision for the future of this institution, and a commitment to support our distinctive mission.
NOTES:

A B C

Leadership and management: Successful experience with leadership and management of a complex university, public or private.
NOTES:

A B C

Academic background: Academic credentials and accomplishments that will earn the respect of the academic community.
NOTES:

A B C

Shared governance: Commitment to uphold our traditions of shared governance with faculty, staff, and students; a collaborative and collegial leadership style.
NOTES:

A B C

Communication skills: Ability to communicate openly and effectively with a range of audiences, internal and external.
NOTES:

A B C

Public advocacy: Ability to act as a campus advocate with state and federal legislators, and to advocate for the many ways that the institution enhances the cultural, intellectual, and economic strength of the people of the state and region.
NOTES:

A B C

Fund-raising: Success in attracting private funds for institutional and program support.
NOTES:

A B C

Diversity: Commitment to support and enhance the diversity and cultural awareness of the student, faculty, and staff populations.
NOTES:

A B C

Personal qualities: Integrity, intellectual curiosity, compassion,   A B C
resilience, energy, and a sense of humor.
NOTES:

Overall rating of this candidate:

        A (strong) _____
        B (moderate) _____
        C (weak) _____

Appendix I:
Reference Questions

CANDIDATE NAME: _____

REFERENCE NAME: _____
    Position: _____
    Institution: _____
    Phone number: _____

Caller: _____
Date of call: _____

Begin by describing the institution and the position; for example:

> The University of _____ is a private research university rated among the 50 best national universities. There are approximately 9,000 undergraduate and 6,000 graduate students, and almost 700 faculty. The president works with the board of trustees to establish vision and direction, and has major responsibility for attracting the resources that make it possible to fulfill that vision.

Remember that not all of these questions can always be asked; focus on the areas in which the reference seems to have most knowledge of the candidate, and/or the areas that are the greatest potential concerns about this candidate.

QUESTIONS:

Candidate relationship: How long have you known this candidate, and how have you worked together?

Key accomplishments: Can you describe some of _____'s major accomplishments?

-
-

Strengths and weaknesses: How would you describe his/her strengths and weaknesses? If no weaknesses are mentioned, ask whether there are any areas in which he/she is less skilled or experienced, or needs to develop more skill or experience.

-
-

Leadership/management style: How would you describe _____ as a leader? Has he/she been effective in selecting and developing an administrative team? How does he/she manage his/her areas of responsibility (e.g., planning, budgeting, supervising staff)? Can you think of a time when he/she has made a controversial decision and describe how he/she handled it?

-
-

Fund-raising: Our president will be asked to lead an upcoming $1 billion capital campaign. How would you describe _____'s work as a fund-raiser? What can you tell us about how he/she works with donors, and how donors respond? Are there any especially remarkable gifts in which he/she played a major role?

-
-

Shared governance: We are interested in how _____ works with key groups and individuals on campus. How does _____ engage others in decision making, especially his/her senior leadership team, and the leadership groups of faculty, staff, and students? How does he/she work with the board?

-
-

Student relationships: What would students say about _____? Is he/she especially well known to students? In what ways is _____ involved in issues of undergraduate education? How about graduate education?

-
-

Academic values: As you think of a range of important academic values (e.g., excellence, academic integrity, academic freedom) are there any particular values that _____ is associated with in your mind? Can you describe a situation in which _____ had to deal with a difficult issue that reflect these values?

-
-

Diversity: What kind of work has _____ done to strengthen diversity, and how successful do you think it has been? (Try to get examples that have to do with students, faculty, and staff.) Can you think of situations in which _____ has collaborated with people of diverse backgrounds? Has he/she ever mentored someone of a different background?

-
-

Interpersonal relations and communication style: Can you describe _____'s way of communicating? Can you describe a situation in which he/she had to listen with particular care to learn about a complex situation and then, following a decision, explain it to critical audiences? How do off-campus people typically respond to him/her? How successful has he/she been in working with donors? Examples would be very helpful.

-
-

Visibility: Has _____ been effective in bringing visibility to the programs in her/her area, or heightening their stature and recognition?

-
-

Concerns: Are there any concerns that we should know about? Is there anyone else to whom I should speak to get a different perspective on _____?

Overall recommendation:

CALLER'S OBSERVATIONS: What is your appraisal of the reference's level of enthusiasm and credibility?

Please send your completed reference to _____ via e-mail by 5:00 PM on
_____. He will post the references on the search Web site the following
day so that others can review it in preparation for our meeting on _____ at
_____ PM.

Appendix J:
Campus Response Sheet

UNIVERSITY OF _____
SEARCH FOR PRESIDENT

CAMPUS RESPONSE SHEET

Thank you for providing your appraisal of this candidate. Your response will be reviewed by the Search Committee as it prepares its recommendations. Please comment on each of the following broad areas of qualification, and indicate your overall responses. Please use examples, and additional pages if necessary.

- *Leadership,* including commitment to our mission, vision for the future, ability to lead the strategic planning process, and successful experience with shared governance.
  COMMENTS:

- *Management skill,* including financial skills, the ability to make difficult decisions with good judgment, and the ability to build a strong leadership team.
  COMMENTS:

- *Resource development,* including the ability to attract philanthropic contributions, and to secure public financial support.
  COMMENTS:

- *Personal qualities,* including strong communication skills, integrity, and energy.
  COMMENTS:

Overall appraisal of this candidate:
  VERY STRONG CANDIDATE: _____
  GOOD CANDIDATE: _____
  INADEQUATE, COULDN'T DO THE JOB: _____

Additional comments:

Your name (optional): _____

Please check your primary status:
  Faculty member _____ Alumna/alumnus _____ Student _____
  Board member _____ Administrator/staff member _____ Other: _____

Thank you. Please return your comments directly to_____,
Committee chair, at (e-mail address) by _____.

Appendix K:
Role of Spouses and Partners

FACTORS TO CONSIDER ABOUT A PARTNER'S ROLE DURING THE RECRUITMENT OF ASSOCIATION OF AMERICAN UNIVERSITIES PRESIDENTS AND CHANCELLORS

The Executive Committee of the AAU, in collaboration with the AAU Partners, offers the following factors for the consideration of AAU institutional governing boards. We believe it is important for governing boards to:

1. Recognize that *if* an AAU President/Chancellor has a spouse/partner (hereafter referred to as Partner), the partnership the pair will bring to an institution needs to be openly discussed. Communication is essential before a commitment is made to enhance their ability to serve the institution well.

2. Acknowledge that the Partner may already have an existing full or part-time career, job, or volunteer commitment. Universities have been better at dealing with an academic Partner's need for a position within the institution than with Partners who come with other backgrounds.

3. Advise the prospective Partner during the recruitment process of the hopes and expectations the Board has for the role of the Partner. Offer the opportunity, where appropriate, for the prospective Partner to meet with university officials and members of the Board for clear communication and understanding about possible arrangements.

4. Consider offering a Partner interested in such an official arrangement, an assignment in her/his role as Partner; this assignment could include a titled position with a position description, salary, and/or benefits, that would be funded as the institution deemed appropriate, either through direct funding or through a university's foundation. Over a quarter of AAU institutions have such arrangements with their President's/Chancellor's Partner.

5. Institutionalize an appropriate support structure for the Partner, beginning in the transition period, to assist him/her in fulfilling the requirements of his/her

assignment to knowledgeably represent the university in internal and external contexts, work with donors and alumni, and/or plan and carry out events at the official residence or elsewhere as part of institutional advancement.

6. Recognize potential areas of initiative and involvement. The Partner's role, if mutually agreed upon by the Board and the Partner, may include one or more of the following:

A. Alumni Affairs and Development

- Supporting university relations
- Fundraising locally, nationally, and internationally

B. University Relations

- Assist with official events for faculty, trustees, donors, alumni, community, students, political figures, and guests of the university
- Promote university programs and events
- Provide support for university programs and initiatives.

C. Community Relations

- Leadership in community organizations
- Public speaking
- Board memberships
- Participation in civic events
- Community involvement

D. The Official Residence as Used for University Advancement

- Assist in the successful execution of official events.

Approved by the Partners Executive Committee—April 2006

Source: AAU Web site; http://www.aau.edu/aau/guidelines.pdf

BIBLIOGRAPHY

Association of Governing Boards of Universities and Colleges. *Presidential Search Guidelines and Directory*. Washington, DC: 2005.

Atwell, Robert, and Barbara Wilson. "A Nontraditional President May Fit Just Right." *Trusteeship*, Mar.–Apr. 2003, 24–28.

Atwell, Robert, Madeleine F. Green, and Marlene Ross. *The Well-Informed Candidate: A Brief Guide for Candidates for College and University Presidencies*. Washington, DC: American Council on Education, n.d.

Bartlett, Thomas. "What Went Wrong With Boston U's Presidential Search." *Chronicle of Higher Education*, Nov. 14, 2003.

Basinger, Julianne. "A Paycheck for Presidents' Spouses?" *Chronicle of Higher Education*, Sept. 22, 2000

Corrigan, Melanie E. *The American College President*. Washington, DC: American Council on Education, 2002.

Cotton, Raymond D. "Firing the President." *Chronicle of Higher Education*, Mar. 11, 2005.

———. "Paying the President's Spouse." *Chronicle of Higher Education*, May 23, 2003.

Dowdall, Jean. "Don't Turn Off Good Candidates." *Trusteeship*, Jan.–Feb. 2004, 24–27.

———. "Adjusting to a New President." *Chronicle of Higher Education*, May 2, 2003.

———. "Courting Elusive Candidates." *Chronicle of Higher Education*, Feb. 11, 2005.

———. "Executive Searches at Religious Institutions." *Chronicle of Higher Education*, Apr. 5, 2002.

———. "Haunted by the Past." *Chronicle of Higher Education*, May 7, 2004.

———. "Haunted by the Past, Part II." *Chronicle of Higher Education*, June 4, 2004.

———. "How Trustees View Presidential Compensation Issues." *Chronicle of Higher Education*, Nov. 14, 2003.

———. "Interim and Internal." *Chronicle of Higher Education*, Dec. 3, 2004.

———. "Telling Key People That You're a Candidate." *Chronicle of Higher Education*, July 27, 2001.

———. "The Next Big Step: From Chief Student Affairs Officer to a Presidency." *Leadership Exchange* 1 (2003): 9–11.

———. "The President's House." *Chronicle of Higher Education*, June 3, 2002.

———. "Unusual Administrative Career Moves." *Chronicle of Higher Education*, Aug. 23, 2002.

Estes, Nick. "State University Presidential Searches: Law and Practice." *Journal of College and University Law* 26, no. 3 (Winter 2000).

Fisher, James L. *The Board and the President.* New York: American Council on Education and Macmillan Publishing Company, 1991.

Funk, R. William. "A Presidential Search Is Opportunity Knocking." *Trusteeship*, Sept.–Oct. 2005, 18.

Gladwell, Malcolm. *Blink: The Power of Thinking without Thinking.* New York: Little, Brown and Company, 2005.

Greenberg, Milton. "A Reality Check on Presidential Searches." *Trusteeship*, Sept.–Oct. 2002, 14–16.

Guardo, Carol J. "An Interim President Sets the Stage." *Trusteeship*, Mar.–Apr. 2006, 29.

Hearn, James C., and Michael K. McLendon. "Choose Public-college Presidents in the Sunshine, but Know When to Draw the Shades." *Chronicle of Higher Education*, July 9. 2004.

Jacobson, Jennifer. "Professors on Presidential Search Committees." *Chronicle of Higher Education*, July 31, 2002.

———. "When the Former President Hangs Around." *Chronicle of Higher Education*, Sept. 26, 2002.

Khurana, Rakesh. "Finding the Right CEO: Why Boards Often Make Poor Choices." *MIT Sloan Management Review* (Fall 2001): 94.

Lapovsky, Lucie. "The Best-Laid Succession Plans." *Trusteeship*, Jan.–Feb. 2006, 20.

Marchese, Theodore J., and Jane Fiori Lawrence. *The Search Committee Handbook: A Guide to Recruiting Administrators.* Sterling, VA: Stylus Publishing LLC, 2006.

Martin, James, and James E. Samels & Associates. *Presidential Transition in Higher Education: Managing Leadership Change.* Baltimore, MD: The Johns Hopkins University Press, 2004.

McLoughlin, Judith Block, and David Riesman. *Choosing a College President: Opportunities and Constraints.* Princeton, NJ: The Carnegie Foundation for the Advancement of Teaching, 1990.

Moore, John W., with Joanne M. Burrows. *Presidential Succession and Transition: Beginning, Ending, and Beginning Again.* Washington, DC: American Association of State Colleges and Universities, 2001.

Neff, Charles B., and Barbara Leondar. *Presidential Search: A Guide to the Process of Selecting and Appointing College and University Presidents.* Washington, DC: Association of Governing Boards of Universities and Colleges, 1992.

Perry, Robert Hastings. "The Art and Science of Reference Checking." *Trusteeship*, Nov.–Dec. 2004, 29–32.

———. "When Times Call for an Interim President." *Trusteeship*, Mar.–Apr 2003, 29–32.

Pulakos, Elaine D., and Neal Schmitt. "Experience-based and Situational Interview Questions: Studies of Validity." *Personnel Psychology* 48 (1995): 300.

Sample, Steven B. *Annual Address to the Faculty, 2005.* Los Angeles: University of Southern California, 2005.

INDEX

About the Author

JEAN A. DOWDALL, Vice President at Witt/Kieffer, Oak Brook, IL, is a consultant to colleges and universities in their searches for presidents and other senior officers. She holds a Ph.D. in sociology from Brown University. Dowdall has supported over 100 searches for senior officers in colleges and universities. Before becoming a consultant, she held administrative posts in higher education, including dean of arts and sciences, VP of academic affairs, president, and trustee. She has written numerous columns for the *Chronicle of Higher Education*, offering search advice for candidates and search committees.